DAWN OF REVELATION

ISBN 979-8-89383-662-2

DAWN OF REVELATION
THE BOOK THAT JESUS WROTE

ROBERT J. POLLICK

CONTENTS

A PARAGON OF CHRISTMAS
BY ROBERT E. FAUST

I cannot help but wonder
How the shepherds felt that night.
When the darkness of the earth was beamed
With heaven's brightest light.

With the angel stepping from the clouds
To speak to men on earth,
Telling the glad tidings
Of the blessed Savior's birth.

The angel said they'd find Him
In the town of Bethlehem.
But many times I wonder
What it meant to each of them.

And how did they determine
Which shepherds were to go
To see our Lord who came to earth
Two thousand years ago?

And I wonder how the shepherds felt
Who had to stay behind,
Missing the greatest event
To come to all mankind?

But there were those who had to stay
And watch the sheep that night,
For sheep without a shepherd
Could be a hopeless sight.

And so it was on Christmas
So many years ago.
Sorne had followed the star,
But others did not go.

But now another Christmas dawns,
And Jesus beckons, "COME,"
To every child of every race,
To every dad and mom.

To you my peace I leave with you,
To you my peace I give,
And though you may be lost in sin,
Look unto me and live.

Yes, Christ is coming back again
For those prepared to go.
For those whose sins are washed away
And garments white as snow.

And so the choice is up to you
Today make up your mind.

The greatest still is yet to come,
Don't be left behind.

ACKNOWLEDGMENTS

MY DEEPEST APPRECIATION TO ...

The many people who have been a part of my life during my ministry.

One lady who has since gone to be with the Lord is Elizabeth Reali. Her father was the man who posed for the statue "The Thinker." She was one of my first church members.

There have been many who have been a part of my early life to whom I am very grateful to have known. One of the grandest persons would have to be my mother, Anna Pollick. I have never met another person with the faith and determination she had in this life.

This dedication page could never hold all the names of those who have been very dear to me. People you meet along the way become a part of what you become in the future.

Clara Randolph was another grand woman who I met along this Christian walk. She was the first Christian I ever met. She was my mother-in-law and went on to meet the Lord some years ago. One day, I asked the Lord, *"How is it, Lord, that you have such beautiful people in this terrible world? And how did they become like that?"*

It seemed as though the Lord permitted me to know a special secret. These people are so lovely because they all have a part of Jesus within their lives. And then my thoughts went on, as beautiful as these people are, when you see Jesus, you will see total beauty. You now see in part what you shall one day see in total perfection.

I especially wish to dedicate this book to my two friends I have known the longest in this life. One is Robert E. Faust, and the other is Valmarie Hummert. These two have been and still remain my dearest friends. They traveled with me to church meetings and to gospel meetings we had on television and radio. They helped me put meetings together. They sang with me on streetcorners. We had and still have a great relationship. I want to thank Bob Faust and Val Hummert for being my closest and oldest living friends on planet Earth. God bless them both.

In my early years, I was permitted to sing in the Kathryn Kuhlman choir. Many of those people were instrumental in my going into the ministry. Miss Kuhlman has also gone on to be with the Lord.

My final dedication is to Jesus. How great a Lord is He that when people who just touch Him become so beautiful. Folks, we have a great future because Jesus has opened it for us to be with Him. May God bless you as you read this book.

Pastor Bob Pollick

PREFACE

Wherever we go, whatever we do, we will always be within God's parameters. In Revelation 1:3 it says, *"Blessed is he that reads, and they that hear the words of this prophecy, and keep those things that are written therein; for the time is at hand."* Going into the book of Revelation is as the Bible proclaims blessing. I can only give what was given to me to understand. There are many things that I do not understand, but I have given them to you joyfully.

What is written here has not been taken from other books. It has been gotten only while in prayer for wisdom from God. I hope this book will permit you to see spiritual things more clearly. The book is written for those who hunger for more truth. Our country is engaged in a great war at this present time. It is not an accident but a part of God's plan. With that said, let us go on to Revelation.

CHAPTER ONE

JOHN AND THE CHURCHES

John was an apostle of Christ. He knew Jesus as he healed and taught. John knew Jesus as a close personal friend. He saw His sufferings and His workings. Up to this point, he never met Jesus as the Alpha and the Omega. Jesus tells John to write in a book what he is about to see. So what is written is not guesswork but John's testimony as to what he was actually seeing. So, we see Revelation as a book that is a "hands-on" experience. The book begins with the words "The Revelation of Jesus Christ." Repeat those words. "The Revelation of Jesus Christ." Jesus is not only talking to John. He is talking to us!

In verse 12, John reports, *"I turned to see, and I saw seven golden candlesticks."* Verse 13 says, *"I also saw one like unto the Son of Man."* What I see here is that John is trying so hard to make sure he is telling what he sees. Not only does he see Jesus, but also the Lord places His right hand on John. John says, *"When I saw Him, I fell at His feet as dead."*

Two things that Jesus does here are:

1. He touches John.

2. He assures him He has the keys of Hell and of death.

As He touched John that day, all fear was removed from John. As Jesus touched him, He said, *"Fear not."* And he lets him know that there is no need to fear either death or hell. John is about to see the "forever life" and what it is really like in heaven.

There are three important things to remember as we leave the first chapter of Revelation: the things that were, that are, and the things that shall be. Jesus tells John and us that Revelation is not only the far future, but it also shows the past and present time.

Jesus said, *"I am He that was dead,"* reflecting the past, *"that lives,"* reflecting the present, *"alive forevermore,"* reflecting the future."

When we find the nuggets within Revelation, you and I will be very "blessed." Our present time is here in God's Word. Nothing is happening without God's knowledge or His permission.

Chapter two talks about the seven churches that were around in John's time. These churches were of a type of spirit, and they left behind them the type of spirit that was going to continue in different church ages. These churches were the birthplaces of future churches.

Jesus gives instructions for the churches to get rid of the bad and promote the needed things. Churches are supposed to be spiritual and not worldly. They are supposed to go after those things described to the churches. Here is a list of the seven churches of Revelation, along with what Jesus told them to strive for:

1. Ephesus, return to your first love.
2. Smyrna, be faithful unto death.
3. Pergamos, go after the true doctrines of Christ and don't let the false teachers infiltrate the church.
4. Thyatira, keep going after doing His works and hold fast until He comes.
5. Sardis, leave formality and go after life. Don't be a fake.
6. Philadelphia, keep his Word. Do not deny His name.
7. Laodicean, go for the true riches. (This church went for worldly riches and money.) And open the door for Christ to come in.

One of the problems today is that the church has become a worldly business instead of being about the Father's business. Jesus said, *"Get the gold I have."* We within the church need to go back to God's ways. Too many people are using God to get to worldly gold. Let us go on to what is about to happen next on the worldly scene.

First, let us know that everything God shows us is not to frighten us but to give us more hope. The tribulation period is not to show how powerful the devil is but to show how God is going to win. And also how limited Satan is, despite the fact that to us, he may seem big. To God, the devil is just another loser.

CHAPTER TWO
GOD VERSUS SATAN

L et us now go to Revelation 4:1, where it says,

"I looked and a door was opened in heaven, and a voice spoke to me and said, 'Come up hither.'"

This is the way it will be at the rapture. A voice will speak to us personally. *"Bob, Tom, Kathy."* Each person will hear the call. *"Come up hither."* And hither we will go.

The Bible says we will have an immediate change. 1 Thess. 4:16 indicates that the Lord Himself will descend from heaven with a shout and with the trump of God. This is the day of Revelation. Some folks think Revelation is tribulation. Not so. Tribulation is only one of the future fates that it is talking about. But this fate is not for the people of God. The part of Revelation that belongs to the people of God is the victory times.

As an example of the victory, I wish to take a moment

to disclose one tragedy that happened in a city where I had a church at the time. Every statement is accurate and on record within the city of Clairton, Pennsylvania.

I started my first pastorate at the age of twenty-one. I took over a church that had a total membership of four besides myself. After being there a few years, I felt I wasn't seeing much accomplished. So, I started doing much praying. I wanted to enjoy God's presence and be in the company of other Christians who were praising God. During these times, our city was going through a major tragedy. We had a racial riot in our school, the Clairton High School. Well, I didn't know what the outcome would be. So, I just continued to pray and go about my business. The riot became so drastic that the schools were filled with police. One day, I was going past the high school to get to my destination. As I went past, I heard someone say they were throwing kids out the window. Some were getting hurt. As I proceeded to go past the school, I felt a tug on my heart: *Go into the school.*

I thought, *'How dumb am I becoming?'* I wasn't going to let this thought remain in my head, so I continued going past the school.

Once again, the thought pierced my mind. *'Go into the school.'* I asked myself a question: *'Why am I thinking this? If I go into the school, they will, at best, beat me up.'* After this kind of thinking ran through my mind for the third time, I said, "*Lord, if this is You, help me, for I am going to go into the school. If this is just me being stupid, please protect me. Remember, Lord, my ignorance. I believe I'm doing this for You.*"

Well, I started to walk into the school. I didn't know what I was going to do if I made it to the school. Let alone know what to say if anyone said anything to me.

I got to the top of the stairs outside the school and was

immediately surrounded by a group of very tall students. Now, I must say I am a white person. And the students that stopped me were black. They asked me a reasonable question. They asked, *"What are you doing here?"* I didn't have time to even think of an answer. So I said, *"I am a pastor and came to help you find an end to your problems."* They asked, *"How are you going to do that?"* I replied, *"Only God can settle this problem."* One boy then asked, *"How can I let God help us when I don't even believe in God?"* I began to pray silently, *'My God, help me. I'm getting deeper into trouble here.'*

And God Almighty kept His hand on me. The next thing I said scared me to pieces because I was just stalling for time to get out of this mess. I didn't even know what I was saying. I said, *"I can prove to you in one minute God is real."* I didn't even know how to prove anything! One boy looked at his watch and said, *"Okay, Rev. You have one minute, and that's it."* Needless to say, I had to think fast!

The only thing I could think of was to start to pray. So I said that only God could prove Himself. I told them I wanted them to give me one minute of prayer- all of them. There were about six boys around me, and I was the shortest of them all. And they had me surrounded and hidden from sight. I didn't know at the time, but these boys were the leaders of the black group! I asked them to join in prayer and hold hands. They did this. And I prayed for God to make Himself real to each one. It was a short prayer, but my whole heart was in it. As we let go of hands, one boy exclaimed, *"Wow! I felt something!"* He, previously the skeptic, said it went right through him.

The next boy said, *"I felt that!"* Every boy there said they felt something go through them. Later in this book, I will relate the entire outcome of this experience. This is also a part of Clairton's records.

In the book of Revelation, we see the problems that will befall the unbelievers. But the believers will be having victories. I want you to know I ended up having a great time with these boys. They hugged me. I hugged them. We praised God. The people on the outside were fearful. We were happy!

John said in Revelation 4:21, *"I was in the spirit, and I saw Him."* If we are in the spirit now, we won't be involved with the turmoil occurring on earth. Verse 4 says, *"There are 24 elders, sitting clothed in white raiment."*

These 24 elders represent the Old and New Testament leaders, the twelve tribes of Israel and the twelve apostles. In the fifth verse, the seven lamps are continuously bumping. God's Spirit is always a fiery presence.

God is *all life.* There is no darkness, dormancy, or death in Him. In God, there isn't any depression. No sadness. God does not live in the dumps. *He is God.* But just to show that God never changes, in the sixth verse, we see lightning and thundering and voices coming out of the throne. This is the telling of God sending out messages to earth to the people, even warnings to the devils, *"Stay away from His people."* We will never know on earth all the things God has protected us from. The devil wants to sift you. Jesus said, *"I have prayed for you."*

The devil and others want to hurt you. But God has

warned them to stay away from you. I say again, we will never know how many times God has protected us on this earth.

In verses 7, 8, and 9, there are four beasts.

These are the highest angels of God who have six wings and are full of eyes before and behind them. They represent the creations of God. The docile calf, the powerful lion, the man, and the eagle, who has sharp eyes that can see with ease, are showing intelligence. The eagle also soars upward. These four creatures also represent a part of what Christ is represented as:

1. He is called the lion of Judah.
2. The calf is a representation of the Sacrificial Lamb. He came gentle as a lamb. The calf was also given for a sacrifice.
3. The third beast is man, and Jesus is called the "Son of Man."
4. The fourth is a flying eagle. *"But they that wait upon the LORD shall renew their strength; they shall mount up with wings as eagles; they shall run, and not be weary; and they shall walk, and not faint."* (Isaiah 40:31)

The Bible says that Jesus will cover His people with His wings. He also rises as the eagle. These angels are constantly before the throne of God. They never sleep. Every time they go around the throne of God, they watch and see things that no one else has seen yet. Around God's throne, many things happen. God is always creating new things. Going into new places.

"Behold," God says, *"I make all things new."*

He makes new people out of the old people, changing their hearts. One of the outstanding things these angels do is give glory to God. They are very close to God and see what he < does and give glory to God. As they give Him glory, the 24 elders also give immediate glory to God. These angels close to God are always seeing and raving about the greatness of God. This is causing great excitement in heaven. We can never know what it is like to have victory after victory.

This is what is happening. They see the outcome of things God is doing, and they come back praising God each time. Even the angels marvel at God's power and creations. Revelation shows how heaven is filled with positive and exciting times. This is better than anywhere we have ever been. There will be no more liars here. No pretense. No fakers here. If anyone says they love you, they mean what they say. There is total oneness here. The 24 elders believe with joy what the angels say. They are so overwhelmed they throw their crowns before the throne of God. The emotion here is at an all-time high. And it never stops!

Verse 11 shows the elders praising God for all His creations. Because God is still in the creation business. God likes everything you and I like, even more than we do!

If you are spiritual, everything God likes, you will like. Everything you like that isn't sinful- God likes it, and even more. His pleasure is in your pleasure.

It is hard to please on earth. To tell the truth, God is far easier to please than the worldly are. We ought to be easy to please.

The fourth chapter of Revelation shows the tranquility, the unity, and the power of God to rule the entire universe. In the midst of all God's work, there is constant praise. The best thing we can do is to give God all of our praise.

CHAPTER THREE

SEALS, TRUMPETS, AND VIALS

We now go to Revelation 5. John sees a book. This book is sealed. No person is able to open this book.

According to verse 3, *"And no man in heaven, nor in earth, neither under the earth was able to open the book, neither to look thereon."*

This book deals with man because man is called upon to open this book.

Remember, Jesus called Himself the *"Son of Man."* This book required someone who was pure in heart, thought, desires, and in all of life. Only He fit the description. When our Lord took the book, the elders fell down. They sang a new song. I believe in heaven; there is much singing, and new songs are always being brought forth. There also seems to be a constant celebration. No idle time. No negative happenings or thoughts.

The new songs sung here are songs of revelation. We often wonder for a long period of time why things happen in our lives. Then, a revelation comes into view. The answer we awaited for so long finally appears, and our hearts are stirred with joy. Words of praise come into our minds, but they can never express how we feel inside. Maybe we have prayed for a healing for ourselves or others, and then it happens. Perhaps the finances we have prayed for are starting to come in. Praise the Lord if the person we have been praying for spiritually has just been born again. God is moving in our lives, and we know it. We cannot help but give thanks, but words cannot express how we feel.

I like all types of sensible music. Many say opera is one of the highest forms of music. Opera often features songs of love and admiration. But more glorious than opera are the songs of worship we offer to God. Opera and other forms of music pretend to mean every word and make it sound as though it were reality. True worship songs to God have total reality with no pretense. King David sang to honor the Lord, and many good things happened, including the deliverance from evil spirits. Here in Revelation, a new song is sung to heaven and earth's greatest hero. Jesus takes the book out of his Father's hand to open the pages of the future. Never has this been done before. The future is about to be revealed.

Many times, as I drove alone in my car, a new song of praise and worship came to my mind. I would then sing to the Lord. No one on earth could hear me, but I felt that He was listening to me. When we enter into glory, we will be in the presence of our exciting Lord. I can almost hear Him say to one of us, *"Hello, my beloved, you will never have to worry again. You will never have to cry again. I will now see to all of your needs personally."*

Back to Revelation, the elders are holding vials full of odors; The prayers of the saints fill up heaven with their scent. There is excitement because the book was opened. *"Why Jesus was slain,"* says verse 12, *"to receive power, riches, wisdom, strength, and honor, and glory, and blessing."*

Every creature acknowledges Jesus' supremacy forever. This book shows what is about to happen on Earth. This book is the word-for-word blueprint of the future.

We are about to explore things that were kept secret. The devil doesn't want his plan revealed, but now we know because Jesus opened the book. That's why it says in Chapter 1:3, *"Blessed are they that read, hear, and keep the sayings of this prophesy."* When Satan moves, we will know because we have read it.

In chapter 6, Jesus opens the seals. The seals reveal things that have been hidden. The devil is a deceiver and the father of lies. He wants to appear to come as a peaceful person and a peacemaker. But Jesus shows exactly what the devil is going to do, even before he does it.

The devil rides a white horse, the same as Jesus does in Rev. 19:11. He is an imitator of Jesus. In Rev. 19:12, Jesus wears many crowns that He earned. Here, in chapter 6, the devil has a crown that was given to him untamed, and he goes to conquer and defeat. The seals that we are viewing here are the things the devil has been trying to hide from the people of the earth. But Jesus is bringing them out into view.

The devil is trying to make people trust him, but watch this in verse 3, "the second beast says, 'come and see.'" In verse 4, we see a red horse, symbolizing the blood of people. Here again, the devil is trying to mimic Jesus.

In Rev. 19:13, Jesus has a vesture dipped in blood. But this is His own blood. This blood that Jesus has is the blood that washes sin out of sight. But the devil, in his deceit, is spilling the blood of the people on earth. Cruel blood, causing hatred toward each other. He also carried a sword, as Jesus did. Only Satan's sword is used to go against the Word of God.

In verse 5, once again, the heavenly beings say, *"Come and see."* He is now riding a black horse. A famine is being sent to the earth. This antichrist wears many hats. You never know what he is doing, but all he does leads to catastrophe. He talks about peace, but he brings trouble with him.

Once again, in verse 7, we hear heavenly beings saying, *"Come and see."* The devil's friends, death and hell, follow him. These are enemies of God.

Verse 9 shows the results, which are the souls under the altar crying for revenge. These seals demonstrate that the devil is a liar, a thief, and a murderer.

Rev. 7:4 indicates what John hears. He hears that God is sealing 144,000 Jews. These preach on earth, and verse 9 reveals the results of their preaching- a great multitude of nations, tribes, and families standing before the throne. Verse 14 says that they have come out of great tribulation. They suffered much to make it out of earth to heaven. They must have gone through hunger, for verse 16 tells us no more hunger and no more thirst. And also no more light or heat from the sun. Verse 17 indicates no more tears. Those who came out of tribulation were special to Christ. This symbolizes the last trouble. The devil has provoked Christ to now get ready to strike back at the devil and his followers.

In Rev. 8:1, the seventh seal is opened, and heaven is

silent. It doesn't tell us why. What do they see? Is it Satan trying to proclaim himself as God? I don't know for sure. But we are going into the last three-and-a-half years of great tribulation. God is now calling together His angels to sound the attack trumpets. The prayers of the saints are thrown to earth with voices of thunder, lightning, and a great earthquake.

In Rev. 6:16-17, we see a fear, for they know God's wrath is coming back on them. Remember, as we read, everything has not been written in exact sequence. We see that the devil actually has three-and-a-half years; for now, God sends His reply to earth. There are seven trumpets and seven woes coming from God, and he is sending a double portion back to the devil and his followers.

At this point, we will go to Rev. 12:1. Here, we see a great wonder in heaven. "And there appeared a great wonder in heaven; a woman clothed with the sun, and the moon under her feet, and upon her head a crown of twelve stars." This woman represents Mary giving birth to Jesus, and the woman is now the church of Jesus Christ. The *real church,* clothed with the greater light.

Here are explanations of the symbols that Mary is clothed with:

1. "Clothed with the sun."-clothed with the greater light.
2. "Moon under her feet"-those who join to become a part of His church. Those who came out of the darkness, the lesser light, are possibly the gentiles who joined in.
3. "The stars."-are the apostles.

We see in Genesis 1:16 that the natural sin came first.

Now we see it symbolized in the spiritual sense. In Rev. 12, the birth of Jesus came from Israel. For this reason, the devil has a great hatred for the Jews and the church of Jesus. The devil brought one-third of the angels with him to stop and destroy God's plan and God's people. This wonder is in heaven, meaning God has His church within view at all times.

In Rev. 9:21, God sends plagues on Earth. It is because man refuses to repent. During the last three-and-a-half years of tribulation, God has the angels blow the seven trumpets. This is God announcing the charge against the devil and his followers. God then pours out His seven vials and seven plagues.

CHAPTER FOUR
FALSE GODS AND FALSE CHURCHES

Let us go to Rev. 11:3. The two witnesses that God has here on earth help pour out the plagues of God upon the inhabitants of the earth. They have the power to destroy anything that comes against them.

The witnesses work as Moses did in the Old Testament. Moses brought God's plagues upon Pharaoh and Egypt. Pharaoh couldn't do anything against Moses. In the book of Job, Satan said he couldn't touch Job because God had a hedge about Job (Job 1:10).

Here again, in Revelation, these two witnesses could not be hurt until their testimony is completed. The plagues are sent from heaven, and these two witnesses are used here on earth to cause it to happen. These two will have power sent down from God. When any try to stop or hurt them, the Bible says fire destroys their enemies! Even the devil is helpless against them!

At the end of their testimony, the witnesses are allowed to die. After three-and-a-half days, they arise, and a great earthquake destroys many. What we are seeing is how hardhearted people are without salvation. This earth becomes very cruel during this time period. There is a great separation between God's people and the unsaved.

I want to go to Rev. 17:3, where John says he is carried into the wilderness and sees another woman sitting on a scarlet beast. The woman here represents a church. The beast represents Satan. This church has all the colors of dignity. She is arrayed with an awe about her that even impresses John. The jewels she wears display much rich-ness. Riding the beast reflects Satan taking her wherever he wants her to go. Kings of the earth defer to her. She has a name called "MYSTERY, BABYLON THE GREAT."

"MYSTERY" indicates she has done evil without anyone knowing. She is drunk with the blood of the saints, meaning this false religion is no longer troubled by killing God's people. This is a misleading church, making people think they are going to heaven.

The beast that carries this church, a promoter of hatred, "was and is not." Satan was *with* God at one time. He left God and now is *not* with God. The devil knows how to conduct false worship. He will never be with God again, but he will proclaim himself to be a god. In the end, he becomes the spiritual leader of falsehood. He comes back as a Christ-the Antichrist. He is trying to become what he once was: a spiritual leader. But the devil doesn't want to settle for second in command this time.

Let's look at some verses that tell us about Satan in chapter 14 of the book of Isaiah. Verse 12, "How art thou fallen from heaven, O Lucifer, son of the morning! How art thou cut down to the ground, which didst weaken the nations!" Verse 13, "For thou hast said in thine heart, 'I will ascend into heaven, I will exalt my throne above the stars of GOD: I will also sit upon the mount of the congregation, in the sides of the north:"' Verse 14, "'I will ascend above the heights of the clouds; I will be like the HIGHEST.'"

Now, let's look at verses about the devil in chapter 28 of the book of Ezekiel.

Verse 13, *"Thou hast been in Eden the garden of God; every precious stone was thy covering, the sardius, topaz, and the diamond, the beryl, the onyx, and the jasper, the sapphire, the emerald, and the carbuncle, and gold: the workmanship of thy tabrets and of thy pipes was prepared in thee in the day that thou wast created."*

Verse 14, *"Thou art the anointed cherub that covereth; and I have set thee so: thou was upon the holy mountain of God; thou has walked up and down in the midst of the stones of fire."* Verse 15, *"Thou was perfect in thy ways from the day that thou wast created, till iniquity was found in thee."*

Satan *is* with God in the end times in the sense that he stands in the holy places and claims to be a god. And many believe it. They believe he is not just with God but that he *is* God.

This is the "strong delusion" of 2 Thess. 2:11, *"And for this cause God shall send them strong delusion, that they should believe a lie."* What is meant by Matthew

> 24:15 is, *"When ye therefore shall see the abomination of desolation stand in the holy place, spoken of by Daniel the prophet, (whoso readeth, let him understand)."*

The words just before this verse are "and then shall the end come. "Satan *is* God to those without ears to hear the prophecies.

> In verse 8, we see that *"The world will wonder whose names were not written in the Book of Life."*

All those that follow this harlot and this beast are going into eternity lost. Salvation does not come through a religion. Salvation can only come through Jesus. This false religion is around today. It seeks more and more political and religious power. As we watch, look for the church that attempts to gain control, even over other religious organizations.

I want to take a look at what is happening today. The country of Babylon (or Iraq) has been defeated by America, England, and Australia. Although Iraq has lost the war, it is not destroyed. Next, Syria will be defeated. This false church sides with certain powers in the last days, during the tribulation period. This church is against the Jewish nation. Again, she is working mysteriously.

I want to say what will happen as I read it in the Bible. Syria will be defeated. In Iraq, the Shiites, in particular, will continue opposing the United States. The Bible indicates that Babylon will not only be defeated but also destroyed.

After America leaves Iraq, trouble will begin again.

America is fighting against the enemies of Israel. As I said, Syria will be defeated, and Iraq will be destroyed in the future. Israel will have the land that God promised her back. This false church will be brought out into the open. This is not just one religion, but many religions that will join with this false church.

But as Iraq is destroyed, so will this religious body be destroyed. God always does the physical things first, and then the spiritual things follow. From the beginning, Satan wanted to have a religion of his own. And he has always been trying to duplicate God. He will have three-and-a half years of forcing people to worship him, putting his seal, name or number in their foreheads or hands. But his power will come to an end. Revelation is in progress even today.

The real church started in Acts. The real church takes in all that accept Jesus Christ as Savior, who are filled with the Holy Ghost. The real church will always love God and all of His people, who are the Jews and the born-again believers.

The false church will hate the Jews first, and also the born-again believers. The real church doesn't have to put on airs. The false church is only an imitator.

Watch out for those who reject the power of God, the gifts of God, and the blood of Jesus Christ. Beware of those that put false gods up, such as sorcery. We don't need the devil's powers or trickery to entertain us. We need more of Jesus. Do not watch those movies that promote sorcery. They are not of God and do not belong in the church.

CHAPTER FIVE
PROPHECY FULFILLED

So many people are saying that the prophecy has all been fulfilled so that the Lord Jesus can return. But as we take a closer look at God's Word, we see more things being fulfilled.

One of these prophesies to study is to be found in Luke 21, verse 25, *"And there shall be signs in the sun, and in the moon, and in the stars; and upon the earth distress of nations, with perplexity; the sea and the waves roaring;"* verse 26, *"Men's hearts failing them for fear, and for looking after those things which are coming on the earth: for the powers of heaven shall be shaken."* And verse 27, *"And then they see the Son of man coming in a cloud with power and great glory."*

These verses, along with many others in the Bible, are letting us know when the end time is. Not the end of the world, but the end of this dispensation (the word "dispensation" is explained in depth later in the book).

Let's look at the signs that shall be from heaven. The signs in the sun pointed out here are constantly being spoken of. One such sign we call global warming. There are strong fears about climate warming worldwide. It is considered so bad that the government has created agencies to try to control pollution from going up into our air. Even many inhalers have been banned. The cleaning up of pollution has been given more priority than ever before. Is man able to cope with this situation?

The moon also plays a dramatic part in the Earth. The movement of the water, such as ocean and sea currents, has been attributed to the moon's movement. We don't have the ability to cope with the powers that come from on high.

The Bible also relates to the signs in the stars. Just recently, we have been informed that many scientists are deeply concerned about an asteroid that may hit the Earth shortly. There is so much concern that a group of scientists have dedicated themselves to the attempt to find a way to prevent this from happening. This event is considered not just a possibility but a probability. These scientists are considering a plan, but they are not sure it will work. They claim this happened many years ago, which caused the extinction of dinosaurs.

At this moment, all these things that the Bible talks about are happening. And we definitely know there is great distress among the nations of the earth.

One large grocery chain has closed its video store section down just to make more room for its pharmacy products. Why is that? Because there is so much demand for drugs, billions of dollars are being spent in that direction, and they make more profit on drugs than they do videos, or groceries for that matter. And if you include illegal dope, Americans probably spend more money on drugs than they do on food. The "distress" and "perplexity" mentioned in Luke 21:25 are causing people to be constantly sick.

The powers of heaven are now being shaken. And just before the appearance of the Lord, it talks about the sea and waves roaring. The tsunamis that take place, such as the one in December 2004, are great tidal waves. Let's go back a bit to Genesis and look at what happened during Noah's time.

Luke 17:26, *"And as in the days of Noah, so shall it be also in the days of the Son of man."*

What did happen during Noah's life? People were skeptical. They made fun of Noah. False gods were replacing the God of creation. Sex had become a god. The man was being worshipped and made into idols. Noah went out with the warning and totally ignored it. Men's idols and sex were becoming gods to most people. Sin always writes the same story. It always tries to make people forget God. It always makes someone or something else popular instead of God.

The results always end up the same way. Finally, the tidal waves carne on earth. Water filled the valleys and then the hills. People cried and ran to higher mountains. No more mountains were left to run to. Earth was totally flooded. The tidal waves were much larger than the tsunamis of today. After all, this was a worldwide problem, not just limited to part of the earth.

God used water many times to bring an end to times. As soon as the tidal waves occurred, the end of that dispensation carne. Noah and his family were still alive; the earth was still there. But a new dispensation began. This time it was Noah and his family who made up the new dispensation. The earthly gods, like sex, had been destroyed. Noah and his family ruled on the earth. And God was greatly glorified.

CHAPTER SIX

THE PROMISED LAND

Let us go on to another time after Noah. Moses led the children of Israel to the promised land. Moses was an Israelite and a man who learned many things from God and learned them well.

Moses learned to take time out to praise God and pray. He went to see Pharaoh. Moses asked Pharaoh to permit Israel to worship their God as God wanted them to. Pharaoh declined. God was not permitted in Egypt's land. Public acknowledgment of God was prohibited. God was not permitted in the schools or public places. After all, Egypt was the most powerful nation in the world at that time and must have had requests to respect many gods from many nations.

After many warnings and punishments, the Pharaoh finally permitted Israel to leave, but as they left, he changed his mind and decided to overtake them. He chased them toward the Red Sea. The sea parted as Israel walked in. Pharaoh continued to chase them. This time, he went too far. The waters closed in on the strongest army in the world. The waves came over them. No place to hide. The waves destroyed Egypt's entire army. Egypt's end came quickly. A new dispensation began. The earth was still here, and people were still living on it, but Israel had become the Lord's chosen people on earth. And God was greatly glorified and feared.

If God is not glorified and feared, then fear will dwell in the hearts of the people. Fear of what will happen next. Fear of the unknown. It seems the water and waves were usually the last warnings before a change took place. The next change that will take place is the end of things as we have it now.

There will be three-and-a-half years of satanic powers loose on earth. Notice how things are shaping up. The world's money system is quickly changing. The church, as we know it, is also changing. The power of prayer and the power of the Bible as God's Word seem to be fables to many.

The only time many people have a fear of God is when bad things start to happen. Because of all the mental stress, people are looking to, for example, entertainment for comfort instead of Jesus and the Holy Spirit, the Comforter. Sports stars, movie and television stars and rock stars have become idols.

The Bible tells us that men's hearts will be failing them for fear. Another thing that is happening today is something we laughed at a few years ago. Something that people said could never happen. People joked about the idea that a computer microchip would be placed within someone's hand or head. A few years ago, it was publicized about a few individuals in the Armed Forces who had a chip placed in them to act as an ID. Most laughed at this and said it was just some sort of fairy tale. It is now being taken very seriously. Surprisingly, some people are accepting and promoting the idea.

When the "church age" is over, the "antichrist age" will begin. The tsunami problem that took place hit us all unexpectedly. There came an immediate fear. What next? Is God doing this? Is God mad at the people? Why are little children being hurt?

All these things are part of the Bible prophecy being fulfilled. The sea and the waves roaring over land now take on a new meaning we never saw before. Verses in the Bible now have a different meaning, even for the so-called worldly.

Revelation is happening in today's world. We are a part of God's world. No place to hide except in Christ. If ever there was a time in America to tum to God, this is the time.

I will be going back and forth in the book of Revelation. I want to now turn to Revelation 11:1 through 11:3. The scene is a changing one.

Notice in verse 1 it states to *"measure the Temple of God, and the altar, and them that worship therein."* Verse 2, *"But the court which is without the Temple leave out, and measure it not; for it is given unto the Gentiles: and the holy city shall they tread under foot forty and two months."* (Forty and two months, three-and a-half years that I have spoken of several times previously.)

The court outside the temple is separated from the temple. What we are seeing is that the spiritual part is being separated from the non-spiritual part (Gentiles). The unbelievers here are treading upon the holy city.

God does and is protecting His own.

God sees and immediately brings forth two witnesses and gives them power in verse 3, *"And I will give power unto My two witnesses, and they shall prophesy a thousand two hundred and threescore days, clothed in sackcloth."*

The two witnesses will be protected by God as they continue to prophesy.

Who are these two witnesses? They have been a mystery that has been wondered about by many.

Some think one of the witnesses is Enoch. Let's take a look at Hebrews 11:5, *"By faith Enoch was translated that he should not see death; and was not found, because God had translated him: For before his translation he had this testimony, that he pleased God."*

A translation is when someone is taken to be with God. The person is changed from a physical body to a spiritual body.

Such a "translation" happened a few times in the Bible and will also occur again in what we call a rapture. Those serving God will go to be with the Lord and will be in God's presence during the greatest suffering that takes place during the last days of the earth as we know it. Let us note that Enoch was translated as saying that he should not see death. The two witnesses will die as recorded in Revelation 11:7. If Enoch was one of the two witnesses, then he would have to die, and Hebrews 11:5 would not be accurate because it says he should not see death.

In Luke 9:30 and Matthew 17:3, Moses and Elijah appear with Jesus on the mount of Transfiguration. They have come to console him and perhaps to find out what will happen after His death. Yes, I believe that the two witnesses of Revelation are none other than Moses and Elijah. These two prophets had to face the worldly forces in their day. Both, of course, were dramatically successful. Moses succeeded in removing God's people from Pharaoh's power. Elijah succeeded in removing the false prophets from controlling God's people. In 1 Kings 18:21, Elijah proved the false prophets to be fakers. This caused the people to return to the real God. Jezebel had the true prophets of God killed. But Elijah turned the tables and had the false prophets done away with. In Revelation 11, God gives these two witnesses the power to shut up heaven so it doesn't rain, to turn the water into blood, and to bring plagues upon the earth. The only two prophets who had been given this kind of power from God were Moses and Elijah. Perhaps they were on the Mount of Transfiguration with Jesus because they, too, would die and be resurrected.

To serve the true God, you must remove the false items that remain in our midst. The true believers must worship the Father in spirit and in truth. That's what Jesus said.

Today, many religions follow the money trail even as the world <loes. You may get angry at what I am about to say. Many preachers don't pray for God's leading but only to go where they get the biggest payday. I do understand

that preachers need to get paid. But we also need to follow the leading of the Holy Ghost. If we are to see the salvation of the lost, we need to be where God is. Who is our leader today? Many want to follow where the praise of man is in the largest church building. They want to follow the popularity of man and the trail of money.

Some time ago, another pastor and I started a ministerial meeting in a certain city. It became well attended. But after a while, the clergy of the largest churches asked us to step aside and permit them to be in charge because we were not well-known pastors in this particular city. So we stepped aside and let it go on with them in charge. We were afraid if we didn't, they would try to prohibit the furtherance of it. It did go on for a while but then ceased to exist.

Sometimes, God uses the unknown little people. Elijah stood alone and faced 450 false prophets who had all Jerusalem under their control. That control was broken, and God was once more recognized and accepted.

In Revelation 11:3, these two witnesses have the power to protect and proclaim. If we cannot protect God's people, then we can not proclaim God's Word.

I believe Moses, who led God's children out of Egypt, will once again be called upon to lead during the most crucial moments in history. In Jude 9, Michael, the archangel, contended with the devil over the body of Moses. Michael said to Satan, "The Lord rebuke thee." Why did Satan want the body of Moses? What good would a dead body do for him?

Shortly after my oldest son was converted, he was very interested in finding out about the Bible and asked me many questions. One day, as we were riding together, he asked me what happened to Moses' body and why Satan argued over the body of Moses. My son had recently seen the movie *The Ten Commandments*, and he was curious.

This was a good question, and I wasn't too sure, except that I knew that God had buried Moses. But why did the devil want the body of Moses? I don't like to say anything unless I feel it is of the Lord. At that point, I prayed and asked the Lord to give me the answer.

Suddenly, a complete picture took place in my mind. It looked like a movie film rolling. According to the book of Deuteronomy, chapter 34, verses 5 to 7, Moses died, and God buried him. We know of no other man buried by God. Moses was in perfect health when he died. At 120 years old, he was as strong as he had been in his youth. Natural forces didn't kill him.

I believe that Moses' body remains in this perfect condition today. The devil wanted to see his body decay. God had a purpose for hiding Moses's body. I believe that the body of Moses did not rot but remained touched by the hand of God. Satan knew God had preserved Moses' body, and one day, it would come out of the ground and fight against him. So Satan wanted to destroy Moses' body. But Michael the archangel withstood Satan. All this flashed through my mind in a matter of seconds. I then was able to answer my son's question. Many times, God has given me answers that I feel came directly from His presence.

Much more could be said about these things, but I want to move on with Revelation. Chapter 11, verse 7, says that the two witnesses will finish their testimony. After which they will die. People will celebrate their death.

We have been hearing of some of the world objecting to the celebration of Christmas. It surprised me to hear the great celebration going on when the Steelers went to the Super Bowl. There was shouting in stores. Pittsburgh was in a great state of excitement about this happening. And yet, celebrating anything about God is wrong to many. Something is happening, folks. The change of this world is so obvious. People are going against God because of the tsunamis, the hurricanes, and other devastation. They are blaming God for what is going on. They ask why God doesn't stop all the problems in this world.

I would like to ask this question: WHY NOT THANK GOD FOR ALL THE GOOD THAT HAPPENS? Why don't our politicians and, media and others in power acknowledge God for being around? Why do they take His Word out of our schools and then blame Him for everything that goes wrong? No wonder the tragedies and problems are happening in our world. We have given Satan control in our schools, our media, and even our homes. Then, fear of the future sets in. What will happen next?

These two prophets will rise again as all God's people will. All that have believed and have lived for God will rise again. A voice from heaven calls them to come up hither. After they ascend, a great earthquake hits the city, and 7,000 die.

During the first three and one-half years of tribulation, Satan is causing great havoc on Earth. He is trying to get this world to worship him instead of God. To do this, he must destroy the two witnesses who are standing in his way. But he can't do this because they have the power from God to destroy anyone who hurts them with fire until their mission has been completed. They are here to keep the testimony of God alive on earth. So when the Bible says their testimony is finished, it means they have completed their job.

God now presents other ways to continue His testimony. Remember, God will always have a witness on earth. Today, the Holy Ghost is witnessing. He stirs our hearts, encourages us, and points the lost to Jesus Christ. This is our time to do something for the Lord.

In Revelation 11:15, we see, *"And the seventh angel sounded; and there were great voices in heaven, saying, 'The kingdoms of this world have become the kingdoms of our LORD and of His Christ, and He shall reign forever and ever.'"*

The two witnesses have completed their testimony, and the promised land is near.

CHAPTER SEVEN

THE TRICKS OF SATAN

Let us now look closely at what Satan < does on this earth. We will also see how God counteracts the devil's diabolical actions.

In chapter 12 of Revelation, we see Michael, the archangel, cast Satan and his fallen angels out of heaven. We then see the anger of Satan as he retaliates against God's people.

When I first read this, I thought to myself, *Why did Michael the archangel cast the devil down to earth?* We have enough trouble without Satan coming here literally, don't we?

Then I read in Revelation 12:10 that *"the accuser of the brethren is cast down which accused them day and night."*

Satan had to be cast down from heaven because he accused God's people. Accusations must stop, for the power of the blood of the Lamb has prevailed. Yes, at this point in time, Satan is on earth, literally. But heaven is free of him. On Earth, the battle rages, but Heaven is prepared to come to Earth with all forces and remove Satan.

Note that in the last verse of Revelation 12, the dragon goes to make war with those who keep the commandments of God. Remember in verse 4 that Satan wants to devour the Child, speaking of Jesus Christ. There is no sympathy from Satan.

Revelation 12 also indicates how the people of God overcome the devil. Verse 11, *"And they overcame him by the blood of the Lamb, and by the word of their testimony; and they loved not their lives unto death."*

You can not destroy what is already dead in this world. You can not place fear in the fearless. You can not defeat those who have won and refuse to quit winning. It is those who do not give up, who keep their testimony alive, who will remain undefeated by the blood of the Lamb and by the word of their testimonies. Their testimonies live on because they love Him more than they love the world.

I remember at one point in my ministry in Clairton, Pennsylvania, where the papers headlined the removal of prayer and Bible reading in the public schools. A lady in my church named Val drew up a petition to pass around. This petition stated that all who signed it agreed to keep the Bible in our schools. We immediately took the petition to everyone we could think of.

Every minister in town signed the petition. Almost all business owners signed it. The school officials signed it. The mayor signed it. Other churches joined us in getting names on the petition. Within two days, almost the whole city had signed it.

The school board agreed to permit Bible reading in Clairton schools. A short while later, the ACLU came to town. They only stayed a short while and left. Clairton was the first place in our nation to fight successfully against banning Bible reading in schools. Why? God placed such a great stirring in our hearts to move rapidly in His name. Even members of the ACLU signed the petition. How could they fight something they signed to protect?

Satan can be overcome by keeping our testimonies alive and letting our testimonies be for the glory of God. Satan cannot defeat what Jesus did, nor can he prevent the power in the blood from prevailing.

Remember that planet Earth is still stained with Jesus' blood. There is nowhere for Satan to hide from the power of Christ. So, as Satan fights us on earth, he will find this to be a losing battleground. The redeemed of the Lord live here.

Let us look at parts of Revelation, chapter 13. Let's see what John saw. Let's see what John saw Satan do. Notice that John sees, hears, and alerts the people how Satan tries to trick people into worshipping him.

John says in verse 1, "I stood on the sand of the sea and saw a beast rise out of the sea, having seven heads and ten horns, and upon his head, ten crowns and blasphemy was also on his head." John sees what the beast is really like. Those who are in Christ will not be fooled.

Jesus said in Matthew 24:24, "For there shall arise false Christs, and false prophets, and shall shew great signs and wonders; insomuch that, if it were possible, they should deceive the very elect." Again, true believers will not be deceived.

The Bible tells us that the Holy Ghost is the Spirit of truth and will guide us into all truth. We need this type of direction badly today. The crowns don't fool John; the seven heads don't fool John. Neither does the power, the seat of authority, or the speech of the devil fool John. No, John sees Satan as he really is, full of blasphemy.

The whole world wonders after the beast. The world begins to worship the dragon. In this chapter, we see how the world is tricked by the dragon and the beast. Notice what the cause of the trickery is. People fall for authority even though it is false.

In verse 5, it says, *"And there was given unto him a mouth speaking great things and blasphemies, and power was given unto him to continue forty and two months."*

Many people seem to like to hear blasphemous jokes. The satanic authority makes fun of God and heaven. He will do miracles, even causing the tire to come down from heaven. He will also give life to an image, causing the image to speak and murder all who will not worship the beast.

The demon powers will be very strong on Earth during this time. Notice what is happening here. The devil, while he is here on earth, uses all his authority and powers to cause people to worship him. Notice the difference between him and Jesus. When Jesus was here on earth, the people tried to take Jesus by force to make Him a king. But He refused their offer.

I have often wondered about why Jesus lived so humbly here on earth. No house to live in. No money, even for his taxes. His taxes. Jesus could conquer the planet if He wanted to. He was a king but didn't fight for a kingdom here on earth. He let them crucify Him. I used to wonder why. Why was our Lord so timid? He could have defeated all the soldiers by Himself. He even said he could call ten legions of angels to fight for Him. Why not call for help when going to the cross? Why not destroy all these criminals who were against Him?

Even the disciples thought He was going to deliver the kingdom back to the Jews as Gideon did or fight as Samson did. He said He was a king. Then why not claim your kingdom?

I found the answer in John 18, verses 33 to 36. Pilate called Jesus to him and asked Him if he was the King of the Jews.

Jesus supplied the answer I was looking for, *"MY KINGDOM IS NOT OF THIS WORLD."*

That was it! He was building a kingdom for the eternal world. The devil had to say, as Jack Nicholson said, that this is as good as it gets. Jesus didn't have to settle for a short-term kingdom. His is an eternal kingdom. Jesus refused this kingdom here on earth. What power! Jesus is only passing through this world. He only came here to pick us up. He set a course for us to follow. He came to earth to let us know He would come again and receive us unto Himself. Now I know why Jesus didn't prevent the Jews from crucifying Him. His kingdom is not of this world. Do you worship the real Christ or the false Christ? Beware the tricks of Satan.

CHAPTER EIGHT

THE WRATH OF GOD

L et us continue to examine verses in Revelations 13.

Verse 1, *"And I stood upon the sand of the sea, and saw a beast rise up out of the sea, having seven heads and ten horns, and upon his horns ten crowns, and upon his heads the name of blasphemy."*

Verse 2, *"And the beast which I saw was like unto a leopard, and his feet were the feet of a bear, and his mouth as the mouth of a lion, and the dragon gave him his power, and his seat, and great authority."*

Verse 3, *"And I saw one of his heads as it was wounded*

to death; and his deadly wound was healed: and all the world wondered after the beast."

This beast came from among people or nations on earth. The sea represents the people of Earth. The beast is the antichrist. The leopard represents speed. The feet of a bear represent spoiling everything in sight. The mouth of a lion represents a voice of authority with a loud roar as it spews blasphemies.

Note that Satan already knows how he is going to defeat the nations of earth. He knows what type of weapons to use. Of course, his greatest weapon is deception. In this chapter, John shows how and what Satan is doing. We see all the powers of Satan displayed here.

One of the heads is wounded. I don't know which head it is. But the wounded head recovers. Regardless of the recovery, one thing is noticeable here. Satan is not invincible. He receives a wound to the head. This demonstrates he can be stopped. Jesus could not be stopped, not by man. He had to submit Himself voluntarily to the enemy to be harmed. The devil got wounded while fighting back.

The next beast John sees is in verse 11. He looks like a Lamb but sounds like a dragon. Here again, he is trying to imitate good but has the heart of the devil. This chapter in Revelation shows Satan in full force and power. He is forcing people to take his mark, his name, or his number. This seems to be his most powerful time on earth. Remember this: not only will people be taking his mark, name, or number, but they will also be forced to give their finances to Satan. Rich and poor will have to receive their mark. You can see the world moving toward this era now as little microchips are being inserted into people. As we come to the close of this chapter in Revelation, it states no man could buy or sell except they receive this mark. Exactly what is this mark for?

Let's take a good, hard look at what is going on. It certainly appears that Satan will control all that is happening in the money realm. No selling or buying without Satan knowing about it. People complain about giving 10% to God and His work. Satan will take much more than 10% here. He trusts no one.

Folks, we need to start giving to God's work now while we can. During the time that Satan is in control, I assure you he will try to make certain that nothing is given to the work of the Lord. Many will be saying someday that they wish they had done more. I wish I had given more. This is our time to do things for God now. Some people are saying you only give to receive more back. We give because of what we have received from Him. Giving without force shows true love.

We are being taught wrong today in many places. Today, it is said that if you give so much, you will receive thousands of dollars back. Is this why we give? What price can we place on spiritual blessings? I thank God we will be delivered from so many of the future problems if we continue in the Lord. Many people testify they gave $1,000 and received many thousands back. While I don't doubt that can happen, THAT IS NOT THE REASON I GIVE.

I gave my last dollar many times and never received any dollars back at that time. Here's what I feel. I thank God my blessings are for the future. The real gold that doesn't pass away is coming our way. I have prayed for many years to understand God's Word. To find the hidden nuggets. To me, that is worth far more than worldly riches. I always pray for God to make His Word real to me as I read it. I may not know it all, but I do more than I used to know.

Back to the point that Satan will be forcing people to do things for him. God, on the other hand, lets us do things willfully. As we conclude this chapter in Revelation, I am in awe and desirous to do more for Christ now. I am inspired to love Christ more and thank God to be able to know the wiles of Satan. Let's make up our minds to do more for Christ in this present time. As we go into the next chapter of Revelation, we will be seeing the righteous people of God coming on the scene. Revelation is letting us see what was in the past, what is happening today to cause the future to become what it will be, and how God will win in the future. Many people are afraid of the future. But the people of God find the future exciting. The church of God is in an exciting spiritual place.

In Revelation 14, we take a look at what is happening with those who love the Lord. And what is taking place in heaven?

Verse 1, *"And I looked, and lo, a Lamb stood on the mount Sion, and with Him a hundred forty and four thousand, having His Father's name written in their foreheads."*

This is the same number that John hears about in Revelation 7, where the 144,000 are sealed. But now he sees them in heaven. Heaven is now so unlike Earth. Earth is full of trials, but here, there is much rejoicing. Harps are being played, and new songs are sung. These 144,000 were on earth during the ministry of the two witnesses. They were on earth when Satan began attacking God's people. These are those from the tribes of Israel who Satan hated. These are those who accepted Jesus Christ as Lord and Savior.

They follow the Lamb wherever He goes. They go through the first three-and-one-half years of tribulation and witness to the Lord. In Revelation 7:9, John looks and sees a great multitude that no man could number. In Revelation 7:14, John is told these are the ones who came through great tribulation and have been washed white by the blood of the Lamb. What a job these 144,000 are doing for the Lord!

No wonder they are seen in Revelation 14 singing a song that no man can learn. They did a work for Christ that most were not willing to do.

In Revelation 14:3, they are now before the throne of God singing. It says no man could learn this song that they sing. It also says they were redeemed from the earth. Looks like they had a little rapture of their own.

It certainly pays to serve the Lord. All the trials are not comparable to the future blessings we have waiting for us in heaven. Don't get discouraged, friends. Don't get upset if all our blessings aren't given to us here on earth. Let's save some for the future.

I want us to take close notice here. While all the excitement is taking place in heaven, much more trouble is taking place on earth. Earth is so bad that for the first time, God has to send an angel to preach the everlasting gospel to people on earth in Revelation 14:5. The message is to fear God and give Him glory, for He is coming to judge the earth. During this time, people were unable to preach the true gospel. If the name of Jesus is mentioned, people are instantly killed. As soon as this angel starts preaching, other angels follow him. One angel shouts out to the people on earth that one of Satan's powerhouses has fallen. Babylon has fallen. WAR HAS NOW BEEN DECLARED ON SATAN ON EARTH.

Heaven has come down to earth to fight Satan and his followers. A third angel comes, speaking for the whole earth to hear. If anyone worships the beast or his image and takes his mark in any form, they drink the wine of the wrath of God. For such a short time of troubles, three-and-one half years, they will give up all eternity. The punishment they will face is forever.

Let's not give up now. We only have a short while to go. Verse 12 indicates that here is the patience of the saints who keep the commandments of God and the faith of Jesus. It's so hard to have patience. But we need it to keep going on. Many die rather than give up their faith in Christ.

Angels are now in this chapter pouring down wrath on earth in the form of plagues. The angel of fire comes to earth along with many other angels. During this time, people will know that there is supernatural power. People on earth have been warned not to worship the devil or to do what he says. Now, those who did are receiving what the angel said they would receive. The wrath of God is come! They are now paying for mistreating God's people. They are paying for following the devil and for all the wrong they have done against God. Blood is flowing on earth, not from what Satan is doing, but because God has had enough. Blood flows as high as the horses' bridles.

SATAN IS NOW IN FEAR.

CHAPTER NINE

GOD KNOWS HOW TO DELIVER

I want to reflect on what God did in the past. For what He has done in the past is a testimony for the future.

Many people have fear as they read the book of Revelation. But God considers it a book with which to bless and be a blessing.

In Revelation 1:3, we read, *"Blessed is he that readeth, and they that hear the words of this prophecy, and keep those things which are written therein: for the time is at hand."*

The purpose of the book of Revelation is to be a blessing to those who read and hear the words of the prophecy.

Our life on earth can also be a blessing if we keep His Word and stay close to Him.

I have found in life that one of our problems is that we

don't enjoy the blessings of hearing Him speak to us. Does He speak to His people today? I must say that he absolutely does!

Sometimes, fear steps in to cause us to deny His voice. Sometimes, other things step in to stop us. I mentioned earlier that I would tell the rest of the story of what happened in Clairton, Pennsylvania, during a riot.

I told you in chapter two of this book about how a riot had occurred in Clairton High School. At the time of the incident in question, I was in a hurry to get to a gospel meeting. If I waited any longer, I would miss out on a great time at the Full Gospel Businessmen's Meeting. I really hated to miss these meetings. So that day, I had to go past Clairton High School to get to the meeting place.

I explained how God spoke to me, although I didn't know exactly what was happening at the time. I only knew my heart pounded, and I felt a stirring urge to do something contrary to all my human inclinations. I left off the story by praying with the young men.

Once again, I want to assure you that this is a matter of record for the city of Clairton. Immediately after prayer, one of the young men asked me what we should do next. Without thinking, I replied that we should have a pep rally in the high school with all the students present and let God settle this problem. They agreed but on one condition: no teachers, no police, and no other adults.

I was very inexperienced in this sort of thing, unsure of what actually was happening, and confused about what to do next. My first impulse was to holler, "HELP!" Instead, I thought of a way to get help. I told them I would like to have one other pastor come in with me, Reverend Bill Callaway. They agreed. Reverend Callaway, a friend of mine, was pastor of Mt. Olive Baptist Church.

Bill and I then had to go to the officials of the school and the city. These officials felt totally helpless during this problem. When they heard a solution was possible, they immediately agreed. I will always thank God that Reverend Callaway came with me. There are times when we need other Christians to stand with us.

Reverend Callaway was a great part of God's plan that day. He and I had such unity as a team for the Lord on that great occasion. I don't think a student took off school that day. The auditorium filled up. Reverend Callaway and I first did a little pep talk. We soon realized something dramatic was happening here.

We asked the students to pray with us. They did. None of us knew just what to do. We couldn't say to the student body, "You have to be good." That surely wouldn't do. We couldn't ask, "Who started this?" That would only prompt a heated discussion. Were you ever in a position where you had no idea what to do? Well, in such a time as this, we knew the only thing to do was to pray. And that is exactly what we did. We were not ashamed to admit we were helpless and needed God to intervene.

Next, we asked the students to hold hands and agree with us that we needed the love of God to take over. What then transpired is difficult to describe. Students began crying. An outbreak of love filled that auditorium. Black and white students began hugging each other. Boys hugged boys. Girls hugged girls. There wasn't any preaching going on. No one was telling the students what to do. A kindred spirit had moved on everyone.

Those students had to leave to let others come in. The same thing happened again. No human was in control. I was only sorry about one thing. I wish the teachers and police could have seen what had gone on. Not only them, but I wish the parents could have been there. But I'm sure the parents heard it from their children later. Bill Callaway and I felt as though we were in heaven. I think we experienced what heaven is really like. The school reopened the following day. The officials of the city and the school never said a word to us or asked any questions. We were asked to come into the school daily to act as counselors. Of course, we accepted. During this time, we were given an office, and the students could come in to see us to discuss their problems. This continued for quite a while. Clairton has not had another school riot since that time.

God does things in mysterious ways. Those students are adults now and may even read this book. I would certainly like to hear from anyone who was in the school auditorium the day this happened. Because of the situation, I was given permission to hold a monthly meeting at Clairton High School. During these meetings, a television reporter attended. His name was Paul Long, and at that time, I believe he appeared on Channel 4 news. Paul Long never missed a meeting and brought his camera. The next day, parts of the meeting will be broadcast on television.

Another regular attendee of the meetings was Bobby Baird, the mayor of Clairton at that time. During one of the meetings, Mayor Baird came forward to accept Jesus as his Savior. At the next meeting, he presented us with a petition making March 15 of every year Youth Crusade for Christ Day in Clairton.

Youth Crusade for Christ is an organization we founded for our work. It still exists today. Not only that, but Mayor Baird placed signs at every entrance to the city with these words: WELCOME TO CLAIRTON, CITY OF PRAYER. If you ever drive through the city of Clairton, you can still see the signs.

On that day at Clairton High School, we all saw what God can do. God knows how to solve problems and turn them around for good. I have given names of people in this book, which I could never do if it wasn't the truth.

I say this to those who have started out on the journey with God: don't ever stop working for Christ. It doesn't matter how bad things look. We, who have been born again, are on the winning team.

Let me ask a question of all those reading this. Have you ever asked Jesus to forgive your sins? Some of you are saying "Yes" and that you did many times. But my next question is-did you give Him your life completely? Do you fellowship with other Christians? Do you go to a church where people still give God the glory? Do you read the Bible every day?

Jesus said if you remember Him on Earth, He will know you that day. If we deny Him here, He will deny us there. As we go on to study the book of Revelation, let us do so as born-again believers. As determined Christians who can say, "I am excited about the future, Lord." The Lord knows how many made it to heaven. And He knows how many more have made it to heaven because of you who have accepted Christ and are telling others.

CHAPTER TEN

TRUE FREEDOM

We keep records of almost everything that happens on earth. We know the amount of rainfall in every city and when the warmest and coldest days are. We know each crime that is reported when it drops and rises. We can predict future events, such as when hurricanes will hit land and where. But we don't know everything. God also keeps records. The tsunami in the Indian Ocean the day after Christmas in 2004 caught everyone by surprise. It killed over 250,000 people.

We forget God is still in control. God also keeps records. When we took the Bible and prayer out of public schools, we thought we knew what was best for our youth. Little did we realize the consequences it would produce. In doing so, we were actually saying to God, "We don't need you in our schools, God. We can handle things without you, God." This is the record we sent to God.

When things started to go wrong, such as shootings and riots in our schools, people got very upset and asked why. With all the problems facing our nation today, people continue to ask this same question. Why doesn't God intervene? There are many wonders. Why does God do these things to people? Many questions. Some say that if this is what God is like, we don't want Him as our God.

I started praying for an answer to this question. This is what came to me. When people tell God to leave their area and their schools, God takes His hands off and lets people have their wishes. Be careful what you ask for. When God's hands are removed, the devil immediately steps in. It isn't God doing these things like shootings in schools. He only did what people wanted Him to do. He walked away. When God walks away, the devil walks in. We need to put the blame where it belongs. People got what they asked for. And the devil did it to them.

Look at all the sins around us. Voodoo dolls are being sold in stores. Drunkenness and sex filling our streets. Men are acting like women. Our television, movies, and internet are obsessed with sex. Churches seem to be condoning this by being silent. It seems as though we don't want to hurt the devil's feelings. What we forget is that God is keeping a record.

In the fifth chapter of the book of Daniel, God examined the record of the king, Belshazzar. God sent the king a message written on a wall. That message ended with verse 28, "Thou art weighed in the balances, and art found wanting." Belshazzar was found guilty. There are many examples in the Bible of God examining man's records.

Has America been found guilty? God is keeping the record. No sparrow falls to the ground without God knowing about it. In the book of Revelation, God knows how many from each tribe of Israel are following Him. He even tells the number. There are two different nations in the Bible. One is the Gentile nation. The other is the Jewish nation. God keeps track of both of them. God keeps a record of each individual. Your record, as well as mine, is already in heaven.

On earth, the government keeps track of taxes. On earth, it's about the money. In heaven, it's about helping others. It's about love. It's about being led by God's Spirit. And a record of all we do is kept. The Bible says we have to give an account of every idle word we say. So we see that even every word is kept. When one person hurts another, God knows it. We here on earth now computerize many records. Much information can be put on a very small microchip. Such microchips are now able to control automobiles and many other things. They can find out where you are with a microchip. The microchip can pinpoint problems your car may be experiencing. Now, they want to put microchips inside a person's body. Microchips have been used as credit cards within a person's palm. We think this is something new, but the Bible told us almost 2,000 years ago, in Revelation 13:16, this would take place.

The Bible says Satan would put his mark on people's forehead or their right hand. So what is taking place has been prophesied many years ago. One danger here is that records of everything about us are being kept. The devil imitates God. What Satan is trying to do is to take control of people's lives. He is attempting to stop all worship of God. I believe this mark will be a way of probing someone's mind and to influence a person to do the devil's bidding. We must be alert to all Satan's schemes. Society is being conditioned to accept these kinds of changes and being told about all the good things to be gained from putting microchips in people and such. Only the Bible has warned us of the bad that will result.

In Mark 13:12, we see that during the tribulation, *"Now the brother shall betray the brother to death, and the father the son; and children shall rise up against their parents, and shall cause them to be put to death."*

Why so much hate in families? Satan will cause it by controlling people with his mark and other diabolical plots.

Those who take the mark of the beast, however, it may be implemented, permit the devil to know their every move. Not only will the mark act as a tracking device, but it will be stronger than any drug man has ever tried because a part of Satan enters into that person. People who have the mark have the devil's characteristics in their lives. Satan will push a button and get people to hate each other. Push another button, and they will even kill without remorse. What a horrible situation to be in without love or feelings. Loneliness and fear will be everywhere.

Jesus said if the Son shall set you free, you shall be free indeed. Our freedom is so important. Jesus came to set us free. Satan is coming to place people in bondage. Before the good can come, the bad has to come to the surface and be removed. All the plans of Satan are now coming to the surface. All those whose minds he has infiltrated are now showing who they are. When Jesus started his ministry on earth, He would send people two and two together ahead of him to let people know He was coming to their area.

Now, what we see in Revelation 14 and future chapters is that the angels are coming to earth to let people know He is coming back. When Christ was born, angels delivered the message. When Sodom and Gomorrah were going to be destroyed, angels delivered the message. Now, when God comes after Satan, angels deliver the message. The angels let everyone know the hour of His judgment is come. He is returning!

John the Baptist was sent as a forerunner for Jesus. John said he came to make the paths straight for Jesus to come. The apostles were sent out before Jesus two at a time to proclaim His coming. Now, in Revelation, angels are sent to let Earth know He is returning.

If you will read Acts 1, verses 10 and 11, you will see that the two angels said that Jesus would come back as He left in a cloud. In Revelation 14:14, we see Jesus having a golden crown and a sickle. He is now getting ready to return to Earth as promised, on a cloud. This time, He is coming as a judge. The wicked are being prepared for the winepress of the wrath of God.

The Lord will complete all He has said. It won't be too long before He begins His reign on earth. He has the crown on in Revelation 14. We don't hear anything from Satan now. His voice is stopped. The blasphemies have now ceased.

Folks, I must repeat that we are not to be afraid of Satan. The only one to fear is God!

When I was young, an older boy used to torment me on the school bus. He would call me names and try to humiliate me. This went on for a while until I couldn't stand it any longer. He was a bully, and everyone was afraid of him. On our way home one day, he started humiliating and threatening me again. I knew the only way to stop him was to accept his challenge and fight. So I jumped out of my seat and not only accepted his challenge but also put forth a challenge of my own. I demanded that he step off the bus immediately.

I found out something that day. Not only did he refuse to accept my challenge, but he never bothered me again. I think he figured that even if he won, he was going to get hurt. Satan is just like that. He terrifies people until they turn from Jesus. But Satan doesn't say much when Christ comes on the scene. God prepares the circumstances for Jesus' appearance. Before the good can enter, the bad has to go.

I want to expound a little more on this subject. If you are born again, you will understand what I am about to say. Before we were converted to Christ, we were in a state of sin. We didn't have a desire to serve Christ. We would never tell anyone we made mistakes. We thought in our hearts we were right. If someone did anything against us, we sought revenge. Revenge was alright in our eyes. After all, we didn't start it. We held bitterness in our hearts because of what other people did to us. We would think that if they can start it, we can finish it. Before I was born again, that's the way I felt. If someone did something wrong to me, I wanted to get even with him or her.

The day I was born again, everything I did wrong came to the surface. I was really sorry for all the things I had done wrong. I began to weep and to ask God for forgiveness. Two things happened to me as I began to weep. All the burdens within me left. I call this the bad leaving. Immediately, something else filled my heart. That was Christ coming. Before the good can come in, the bad has to leave.

CHAPTER ELEVEN

VICTORY

God said within His Word to work out our salvation with fear and trembling. We, as Christians, need victory in all walks of life.

Sometimes, it takes me so long to find the solution that I almost lose it. Many answers I have gotten from the Lord took so long that I almost gave up seeking the answers. What I am about to show here is so very simple that I could not find it. There were reasons I was having such a hard time, reasons that I couldn't understand. I could believe in heaven and life after death, but I couldn't find myself accepting that God wants to give answers to our life's needs now.

First, I want to say why I wasn't getting all the victory I needed. I listened to many voices. For the first twenty years of my Christian walk, I said very little. I wanted to hear what others had to say. I didn't feel qualified enough to share my opinions. I was always drowned out by the voices of others. Slowly, I started to listen to what was coming into my mind and heart instead of listening to others. *Are these ideas from God?*

I tried one idea that sounded wrong to most people, but it worked for me. There was something more that I wasn't hearing. I knew God had more to tell me, but I couldn't seem to hear it. I prayed desperately for God to show me what I was missing. I read in the Bible that He knows when every sparrow falls. He even knows the hair on each person's head. What I realized is that we need to do God's will.

Many evangelists were saying that if you want success, you need to send them a lot of money. Others said you need their miracle formula. It is so wrong to fool people. We need to stick with the Bible. Don't do something just because someone else does it. There are people reading this book who need to know how to make sure we are doing as God's Word says.

I'd like to refer to a verse here that constantly pops into my head.

Matthew 7:7, *"Ask and you shall receive. Seek, and you shall find. Knock, and it shall be opened to you."*

Much success hinges on this verse. It took me over twenty years of searching to finally use this verse.

ASK means when you ask, believe God will speak back to you. When you ask God, never get discouraged and quit. When you ask, be prepared to do what God wants you to do. Above all, do not permit negative thoughts to enter your mind. Don't walk away feeling disappointed. Remember, God cannot give you or me negative answers. God is too powerful to lose. If you don't hear from God at first, keep coming back.

God is not a sugar daddy. He will show us how to be successful, but He will not do your work for you. We must be ready to act on what God lets us know what to do. If we don't know how to start, we must look toward what we can do well. Am I a good cook? Can I talk nice to people? Can I help someone in need? Slowly, God will show us what we can do. If you can't do things without getting upset, angry, or jealous, it's time to go back to the drawing board and start over. Now, when you reach the point of hearing from God, it's time to go to the next step.

KNOCK, start knocking and putting to use what we have learned. Do something with what you have learned. In conjunction with this, always remember to give to God your tithes. Next, take time to hear from God and read His Word.

Now let me tell you what I feel God was making real to me. What is the reason you are seeking financial success or whatever it is? Are you doing it for popularity? No, then what is it for? Will you help others because of your success? Yes? Let's go on. Will you forget God if you have success? No. Will pride step in if you have success. Again, no. Now, examine yourself. What is the best ability you have in your life in the Lord?

In 2 Kings, verses 1-4, a widow came to Elisha and asked what she should do because of the situation that her sons were about to be taken from her and made slaves because of her financial problems. Elisha asked what she had in the house of use. She told him and responded to the instructions of the Lord's prophet in faith and obedience. A miracle occurred. It took two things to get the victory. It took hearing from God and then doing something about it.

It took something spiritual, and then she had to add something natural to it.

You and I may differ in our abilities. I believe that every person is someone special. It is so special that God blesses people in different ways. We need to be bold to move forward. When we know what we have felt in prayer, we then need to move on. I felt God was inspiring me with these words: WHAT CAN YOU DO BEST? I began to examine myself until something began to stir within me. I knew something was coming to the surface. Next, I felt I must do it without reservation or excuses. The worldly do everything possible to be "successful." If we are doing something for the Lord, we should do it with all the power and ability we have.

Success in the Lord is out there. All we have to do is to get a hold of it and not let it go. I had a cousin who couldn't sing a lick. All his songs sounded like he was talking. He kept trying and trying to sing. He wanted to lead the singing in church. We all had to sing loudly to cover up his singing, or it would have sounded terrible. One day, he started to lead the singing of a difficult song. As he sang, everyone else stopped singing and let him lead. I have never heard anyone sing that song as well as he did today. Nothing intimidated him, and he succeeded.

What we need to do is to not let people stop us. Don't feel you can't do it if you feel led by the Lord. Don't be a wishy-washy person who gets discouraged every time something goes wrong. People will always tell you it can't be done. People will always try to stop you. Only God will keep us going. People tell me Walt Disney went broke many times before he succeeded. But you're not Walt Disney, you say. People try to put you up against someone with great results and tell you you're not them. I am what I am, but I will be what only God can make me. Too many people want to sleep all day and think success will come in their dreams.

Great success comes only from God.

Of course, it depends on what you call success. I don't believe you have to cheat to succeed. Many times, business people lie and cheat to get what they call success. Sorne people feel the end justifies the means. This is wrong. If God doesn't give it to me, then it's not for me. Remember, God doesn't live in the dumps, so let's live above the discouragements. If we really try to live above the problems, God will help us to be overcomers. If we let everything discourage us, then we will probably always find something to blame our problems on.

Everyone has some sort of talent from God. We need to ask God what it is, and when we find it with God's help, we need to pursue it without quitting. The success we receive will be great. When I feel I'm going through hard times, I think about the folks who really have it tough. Many of the problems we have are small compared to others.

During the first three-and-one-half years of tribulation, it will be hell on earth. Those poor people who want to serve God will have it very difficult. But there will be a time when Jesus will come for all those who are waiting for Him. It is mentioned many times in the Bible.

Revelation 3:10, addressed to the church of Philadelphia, states, *"Because thou hast kept the word of My patience, I also will keep thee from the hour of temptation, which shall come upon all the world, to try them that dwell upon the earth."*

This "hour of temptation" is the tribulation time. Those who keep putting salvation off will have to go through very hard times to make it.

We saw in Revelation 14:8 that that great city Babylon has fallen. The whole world seemed to have loved this city. The angels of God start "cleaning up" with this city. This chapter is the beginning of change and shows how God is moving.

In Revelation 15:2, we read that many have gotten victory over the beast, over his mark, over his name, and over his image. These people did so during the most difficult times Christians have ever had. They are able to overcome. They defeat the beast in all his strength. Now, if they can do it, then we surely can be overcomers now. Why are we so weak?

I hear people say the devil is after them and giving them a hard time. Sometimes I hear people say the devil <lid so many things to them. We can be overcomers. If our brothers and sisters can overcome, so can we. We need a positive attitude. We need to trust God. Those who overcome during the tribulation are mighty warriors for God. They have harps of God. They sing special songs of victory. There is much singing in heaven.

CHAPTER TWELVE

GOD'S WILL BE DONE

Yes, we see the victory coming in Revelation 15. I spoke previously of the seven last plagues that God sends to earth.

In Hebrews 11:10 it talks of Abraham looking for a city whose builder and maker was God. I think that Abraham searched for a city that was made special by God. Do you suppose that Abraham ever imagined that the earth would one day be under attack by God?

As the seven last plagues are being prepared to be sent to earth from God, we see a temple that is called the "Temple of the Tabernacle of the testimony in heaven" in verse 5. Before anyone can enter, the seven last plagues must be poured out. All the bad must be dealt with before the testimonies can be released. These many testimonies will show the great power of God. Testimonies of how God came from heaven to protect His people. Incredible answers to prayers will be revealed.

Jesus told us not to love the world or the things in it. Jesus told us that if any man loves the world, the love of the Father is not in him. None of God's people will be harmed during these plagues. The first vial of plague is poured out on mén who have the mark of the beast. There will come upon those who have surrendered to the beast or the devil grievous sores so bad that they will fill the air with their crying.

Next, the waters and seas will be turned into the blood of dead men. Everything in the sea will die. Then, the beautiful fountains will flow blood, and the rivers will run red. An angel tells us that those who have shed blood now will have the blood returned to them. This has all taken place during the last three and one-half years of tribulation. All of God's people are protected during this time. The sun then becomes so hot that it scorches people on earth. But not God's people.

The unsaved feel that life on earth is better without God's protection. They are finally getting their wish. Little did they know it was the prayers of the saints that kept the wrath of God away. The next angel pours his vial into the center of where Satan rules. The devil's kingdom is filled with darkness and much pain. It appears that God would like to see the people repent because it says that throughout this entire time, people refuse to repent. We are looking at hardhearted people here. They have lived in stubbornness, getting their own way and never caring about others or God.

Revelation 16:13 shows us three unclean spirits of devils coming to gather the kings of the earth together. Notice the imitation-there are three of them, just as there are the Father, the Son, and the Holy Ghost. Here is where Armageddon takes place. This is all happening near the nation of Israel, close to where Christ was crucified. This is where the most suffering takes place. Little do they know

God has led them to this place. God has to bring all the evil out of hiding. Those who side with the devil will come to fight against God. This battle will take place before Jesus returns to earth. Before the thousand years of peace come to earth.

Nothing bad that was done will go unpunished unless they surrender to the Lord. All false religions will be brought into the open. John sees the great religious city, Babylon. As I spoke of in a previous chapter, she is riding on a beast. This warrants some repetition. The beast is the devil. This woman is very rich. She is decked out in gold and with every expensive gem there is. She is clothed in much royalty and beauty. But she rides on the back of the devil. This woman is called "MYSTERY" and "MOTHER OF HARLOTS" in Revelation 17:5. This woman has been mysterious because she is so changeable. She can be for the good, and she can be for the bad. Her final fate is shown here. Folks, we must get off the fence and go wholly for God!

Yes, the woman is called the "mother of harlots." She has killed many good people and hidden that fact. She will take a stand for the powers that oppose God. It indicates in verse 16 that the waters she sits upon are many nations. So, we see that her throne sits upon many people of different nationalities. She is a worldwide power. But she and her power will now be destroyed. The devil uses all kinds of tricks to turn people away from God. He uses world powers, religious powers, and demon powers. This "religion" will be for and against God. She will be for the things that help her prosper.

I want to repeat something I said before about the devil. In Revelation 17:8 it refers to "the beast that was and is not and then will be." The devil was with God. He now is not with God. The devil is now separated from God, but he used to be close to God and lead the music in glory. And as I stated previously, in the last days, many will believe Satan *is* God.

Many people listen to other people instead of God. People make mistakes. I wouldn't want to trust my salvation to any person or organization. You can't start over in eternity. This beast knows how to act like a spiritual being. We think the sun is bright, but in heaven, there are angels bright enough to light up this entire earth. There are some of God's people in false religions. In Revelation 18:4, we hear the Lord call those people and tell them to come out of the false religion. If God is calling them, they must be His people in spite of false religion. God calls them out so they won't be a part of the mother of harlots' deeds.

During the end of the tribulation period, there will be many angels on earth. There have always been angels on earth, mostly unseen. But during this time, they will be seen. Many of us believe in angels, but we do not worship them. There are people who worship angels. God never intended this to happen. I have wanted to see or talk to angels but never have, except possibly once.

This verse from John 20:29 frequently comes to my mind, *"Blessed are they that have not seen and yet believed."*

I have always been satisfied with that. In the following chapters, I will talk about angels and my experiences.

In Revelation 18:2, it repeats that Babylon the Great has fallen. Because it is repeated, it shows that she is doubly rewarded for her evil. First, she has fallen as a false religion, and also, she has fallen as a world power. Twice the punishment for her wickedness. Those who don't care what happens to others and are willing to lead people astray just for the sake of money will be recompensed double. Those who love the Lord will come out from her, for the Lord is calling them out. There will be a mass exodus. Babylon has become the "habitation of devils" in verse 2, and then we see clearly her fate.

In verse 7, we see how wonderful the great whore thinks she is. *"How much she hath gloried herself and lived deliciously, so much torment and sorrow give her: for she saith in her heart, 'I sit a queen, and am no widow, and shall see no sorrow.'"* But in verse 8, *"Therefore shall her plagues come in one day, death, and mourning, and famine; and she shall be utterly burned with tire: for strong is the LORD God Who judgeth her."*

The angels are preparing everything for Jesus to come back to earth and take over. Jesus told us His angels would gather His elect from the four comers of the earth and that the righteous would be placed at His right hand and the sinners at His left hand. In these chapters of the book of Revelation, we see that separation is taking place.

CHAPTER THIRTEEN
ANGELS

There are two kinds of angels- the angels of God and the angels of Satan. When Lucifer left God long ago, one-third of all the angels went with him, as verses 3 and 4 of Revelation 12 indicate. And now we see a great battle between the angels of God and the angels of Satan.

Let us read those verses in Revelation 12. Verse 7, *"And there was war in heaven: Michael and his angels fought against the dragon, and the dragon fought and his angels." Verse 8, "And prevailed not, neither was their place found anymore in heaven." Verse 9, "And the great dragon was cast out, that old serpent, called the Devil and Satan, which deceiveth the whole world: he was cast out into the earth, and his angels were cast out with him."*

Yes, Michael and his angels fought against the dragon

and his angels. Michael is the angel of war. Michael is one of the mightiest angels of God in heaven.

I want to focus your attention on the part where Satan is cast out of heaven. We see that Satan and his angels no longer have a place in heaven. From this moment, they can no longer come home, so to speak. They have been totally kicked out forever. Who takes their place? In 1 Corin. 6:3 Paul says, "Know ye not that we shall judge angels?" Could this mean that man takes over the place where Satan and his angels had been?

Now we know from the book of Job and elsewhere that Satan was the accuser of the brethren. Satan was constantly accusing those who love God. Not only did he accuse Christians, but he also lied about them. He judged man. Now, man will judge him. The Bible says judge not that you be not judged (Matthew 7:1 and Luke 6:37). Satan judged man, and again, now he must be judged. What goes around comes around, don't they say? God's laws apply to all. Those who talk maliciously about others and judge them will end up being judged themselves.

Why did these angels leave God and side with Satan? The Bible does not tell us. I just thank the Lord that we have the opportunity to be born again. One reason that man can be forgiven is because man never invented sin. The man was tricked into sinning. Satan invented sin. Because of this, he can not be reconciled to God. God took into account that man was deceived, and He made a way for man to be forgiven. We must accept this opportunity! Those who refuse will have nothing to look forward to. Those who refuse to repent will be like the fallen angels. To be born again is not something to be taken lightly, nor can we make fun of being born again. As soon as Satan deceived man, God came up with a plan to redeem man, a way to bring man back to Him. That is why Jesus died.

This plan had to be well made. It had to be without partiality. It also had to be powerful enough to stop Satan from claiming guilt on the part of those being redeemed. For this reason, Jesus had to give His life as a ransom for each and every person on earth. There also had to be some force to make a change within those who surrendered to Christ. That force is called a born-again experience. It is so powerful that a person knows a change took place in his or her life. This plan had to be sealed with purity enough to cover all people from the very beginning of creation. It also had to be done by blood because each person had a blood-line from which they came. This impure bloodline had to be changed. There was only one personage in the entire universe who qualified. His name was JESUS, the SON of the living GOD.

Jesus alone had lived eons of time with a pure, unde-filed bloodline. Jesus was pure enough to reconcile hundreds of generations of people back to God. Jesus' bloodline was pure enough to give salvation to every person who ever lived, should they accept Him. The angels of God were so glad to see the birth of Jesus. They came with the news to the shepherds and left with a glorious song.

Angels are now visiting the earth. I believe that angels visited Jesus during his youth. We see during Jesus' trials and tribulations that angels would come and encourage and strengthen Him. We see angels at the tomb of Jesus after He was crucified. They did not intervene, but they were prepared to act if necessary. I believe that the angels of God keep Satan's angels from causing destruction at times. The angels were there when Jesus was leaving earth in Acts 1. The angels confirmed that Jesus would return. They even said how He would return. Toe angels of God continued on earth even after Jesus. I believe, as I have said, that the angels of God are here even to this day.

When Peter was put into prison by the evil forces, angels got him out. When Paul and Silas were accused and imprisoned wrongfully, the angels of God opened the cells. I think that these incidents were to spiritually show to all who had been bound by Satan that they could be released in Christ. In other words, God's power is stronger than all the forces of evil.

Jesus came to release the prisoners of sin. You who are reading this book can find this out for yourself by surrendering to Jesus Christ now! Tell Him you want Him in your life and heart. Ask Jesus for forgiveness. Now, in your own words, begin to thank Christ for loving you. This could be the greatest day of your life.

Some years ago, two women went with me to do some witnessing about the Lord. Val Hummert, Nina Reali, and I went to the Oakland section of Pittsburgh. I felt a compelling urge to go to Pitt University. No one else went in with me. I found myself in the university library. Immediately, I took tracts out of my pocket and searched for someone who would listen to me. The librarian approached me and told me I had to leave. She told me that religious tracts were not permitted and it was illegal to do what I was doing on university property.

While I was prepared to leave, a girl approached us. She told the librarian she wanted to ask me one question and wanted her to permit me to stay long enough to answer. The librarian agreed, and the girl, who said her name was Jane, asked me one of the hardest questions I had put to me. The worst part was I didn't know the answer. Her question was, "Why did God create a Hitler?" Jane was Jewish, and this question bothered her.

I began to pray silently. A thought came to me, and I asked Jane if she believed in God. She answered that she used to believe in God but could not anymore since God created Hitler. I then told her my thoughts on the subject. God never created a Hitler. God created a man. This man rejected God, accepted the devil, and became a Hitler. It was never God's will to create such a monster.

I inquired if Jane wanted to believe in God again, and she said she did. She then asked how she could make herself believe when it wasn't in her. I told Jane that only God can reveal Himself to people. I asked her if she would do one thing and let God make His presence real to her. I suggested we pray together and see what happens, and she agreed. I began to pray, and it was only a minute or so until the presence of God moved on us. I asked her if she felt any different. She began to weep and said that she did. "Jane, I would like to ask you to do one more thing," I requested. She looked at me and replied, "I know what you are going to ask me. I can never accept Jesus."

I then asked Jane if I could pray again and told her she didn't have to say a thing. "If Jesus is real, you will know it, Jane," I said. "If He isn't, it won't hurt you." She gave me permission to pray. I could tell the librarian was about to tell me to leave again because of the way she watched us.

Once again, I prayed for Christ to make Himself real to this young lady. When I finished praying, Jane was really crying. She then agreed to ask Christ to forgive her and to come into her heart. The librarian then told me that my time was up and I had to leave. But I was so happy when I left there! Jane departed the university shortly after that and began testifying to the Jewish community in Philadelphia about Jesus. This became the greatest day in Jane's life, and it can also be your greatest moment. I believe the angels were able to bring a good report back to God that day.

In Hebrews 13:2 it states, *"Be not forgetful to entertain strangers: for thereby some have entertained angels unawares."* We can be entertaining angels without knowing it. Angels are here, and they have jobs to do. Jesus told us, *"I must be about My Father's business"* in Luke 2:49.

God has a business going here on earth, and He has watchers keeping an eye on his business. There are times when angels are visible, and there are times when angels are invisible. Elisha asked God to open the eyes of his servant, meaning himself, and when his eyes were opened, he saw the mountain full of angels' horses and chariots (2 Kings 6:16-17). Sometimes, only certain people can see angels. There are many angels on earth, even as we continue our daily walk. The angels have an interest in God's work here on earth.

They protect God's work. They keep the evil spirits away. They have protected us more than we know.

Angels are sometimes on the scene to bring reports to God. You could be meeting an angel when you least expect it. I remember when my children were young and we were at a fast food restaurant getting a sandwich. When we were ready to leave, I noticed I had a flat tire. So I jacked the car up and went into the trunk to get the spare tire out. I told my children to stay away from the front of the car because it was on a jack. My car was parked in front of a fence. It was a large car, as many were in the early 1970's. As I was getting the spare tire out of the trunk, the car slipped off the jack. At that precise moment, my youngest child, Jeffrey, walked between the front of the car and the fence. Well, the car lurched forward and pinned Jeffrey against the fence.

I couldn't start the car because I was afraid it would really squash him. So I jumped between the car and the fence, along with my eight-year-old son, Bobby, and my twelve-year-old daughter, Lorrie. We tried to push the car backward. The three of us grabbed the front bumper and began to push. To my surprise, as the three of us started pushing, the car lifted up, and we were able to push it backward a few feet, enough to release Jeffrey from the pressure of the car. When Jeffrey was free, he just buckled over and fell down. I picked him up and placed him in the car.

I then hurried and changed the tire. When I started the car, I was amazed to see the car was still in park. I knew at that moment God had sent an angel to help us, even though I never saw him. While we were on our way to the hospital, Jeffrey was unconscious. By the time we arrived at the hospital, he was alert and feeling good. Jeffrey was x-rayed, and nothing was found to be wrong with him. Again, I believe God sent an angel down to help us. I did not see the angel, but I know we could have never moved that car. I believe that many other times, I have been spared from an accident, and it was not a coincidence. It was God. I believe angels will be here on our dying day and take us to God's presence.

CHAPTER FOURTEEN

PEACE IS COMING

T he power of waves.

Psalm 107, verse 25, *"For he commandeth, and raiseth the stormy wind, Which lifteth up the waves thereof."* Verse 26, *"They mount up to the heaven, they go down again to the depths: Their soul is melted because of trouble."* Verse 27, *"They reel to and fro, and stagger like a drunken man, And are at their wit's end."* Verse 28, *"Then they cry unto the LORD in their trouble, And he bringeth them out of their distresses."* Verse 29, *"He maketh the storm a calm So that the waves thereof are still."*

Here, we see that because of the waves alone, people are at wit's end. What people fail to accept is that all the forces of nature are under God's control. Only God has power over the natural forces. It says in verse 26 that the waves can mount up to heaven!

Jeremiah 51, verse 42, *"The sea is come up upon Babylon: she is covered with the multitude of the waves thereof."* Verse 43, *"Her cities are a desolation, a dry land, and a wilderness, a land wherein no man dwelleth, neither doth any son of man pass thereby."* Verse 44, *"And I will punish Bel in Babylon, and I will bring forth out of his mouth that which he hath swallowed up: and the nations shall not flow together anymore unto him: yea, the wall of Babylon shall fall."* Verse 45, *"My People, go ye out of the midst of her, and deliver ye every man his soul from the fierce anger of the LORD."*

Here, Jeremiah is talking about the prophecy of end times. Whenever you hear about the last days, you constantly hear about the destruction of Babylon. Here again, we read of the waves. We have seen what the tsunami in December 2004 did, but worse waves than that will be coming to Earth. This Babylon Jeremiah is prophesying about is the same Babylon of Revelation. This Babylon is filled with graven images and idols. She has done much harm and will be completely destroyed. Again in these verses in Jeremiah, we see God calling the people to go out of Babylon as we saw in Revelation.

Throughout the Bible, we hear about the strength of the forces that we call nature but are actually God's forces. It was water that flooded the earth in Noah's time.

Genesis 7:11, *"The same day were all the fountains of the great deep broken up, and the windows of heaven were opened."* Water shot from under the earth and poured from the clouds above. It took God only forty days to flood the earth. Psalms 24, verse 1, *"The earth is the LORD'S, and the fullness thereof;"* and verse 2, *"For he hath founded it upon the seas, And established it upon the floods."* Revelation 21:1, *"And I saw a new heaven and a new earth: for the first heaven and the first earth were passed away, and there was no more sea."*

NO MORE SEA. Before this happens, there will not only be huge tidal waves but also incredibly severe earthquakes. And volcanoes. Isn't it strange we are fighting for a piece of earth that will be done away with someday? But the new earth will have a solid foundation. No more floods, no more tidal waves. The end of one dispensation and the beginning of another. Those who make it through will be the everlasting generation.

There are three beings within the antichrist regime, just as there are the Father, Son, and Holy Spirit in the Godhead. Revelation 20 and 21 show us the end of all the forces of the antichrist- the beast, the false prophet, and the dragon, which is the devil. Revelation 20:4 says that those who died for Christ will reign with Him for the 1000 years that we call the Millennium. During this time, we will see only peace in the entire world because the devil will be bound.

Isaiah 11, verse 6, *"The wolf shall also dwell with the lamb, and the leopard shall lie down with the kid; and the calf and young lion and the fatling together: and a little child shall lead them."* Verse 7, *"And the cow and the bear shall feed; their young ones shall lie down together: and the lion shall eat straw like the ox."* Verse 8, *"And the sucking child shall play on the hole of the asp, and the weaned child shall put his hand on the cockatrice den."* Verse 9, *"They shall not hurt nor destroy in all My holy mountain: for the earth shall be full of the knowledge of the LORD, as the waters cover the sea."*

We see from these verses in Isaiah that no one will be hurting others during this time of peace. A little child shall lead wild animals. We all will be vegetarians, as the lion in verse 7. Even a snake will not hurt a child, as we see in verse 8. Isaiah tells us in verse 9 that the earth will be full of the knowledge of the Lord. I believe that there will be much training going on during this time, a school for people who enter heaven. Many are saved, but we need to learn more about respecting others, among other things. I suspect there will be a whole lot of Bible study.

People will live to be hundreds of years old during the Millennium. All curses will be lifted during that time. It will probably take 1,000 years of training for people to mature in the Lord. After all, God didn't make heaven for man to go up there and mess it all up!

The events I have spoken of in Revelation must play out before peace does come. You might say that the book of

Revelation must be fully revealed. But rejoice, born-again believers, because peace is coming! A peace like none of us have ever experienced or can possibly imagine.

CHAPTER FIFTEEN

AMERICA IN GOD'S WORD

I do not try to tell people I know exactly what is going to happen in the future. What I am going to do is explain what the Bible indicates is happening at certain times with respect to prophecy. This, in turn, I hope, will let people see the truth of the Bible.

The Bible speaks mainly of the Jewish nation and the Gentile nations in prophecy. The Jewish nation prevailed when it served God. Then, as the Jewish nation faltered, God used the Gentile nations to do His will. The second chapter of the Book of Daniel is all about how God transferred the leadership of the earth from the Jewish nation of Israel of the Old Testament to the Gentiles.

Israel of the Old Testament was to be God's messenger to the world, but Israel tragically failed.

Let me pause briefly to discuss the word "Jewish." The typical dictionary definition of the word "Jew" is a person descended from the ancient Hebrews or a person whose religion is Judaism. The nation of Israel as we know it today is a Jewish state, both ethnically and religiously.

Over three-fourths of the residents of Israel today are considered to have descended from the ancient Hebrews and practice Judaism. Of course, you also have a much lesser number of Muslims and Christians in Israel, but the point to remember is that it is still the Jewish nation of the Bible, God's chosen people. But Israel will not return to its former glory until Jesus returns.

As Israel is in the Word of God, so is America. So are other nations. America is not mentioned nearly as much as Israel, one reason being that America does not come into power until the latter time. There are prophecies for Israel, and there are prophecies for the Gentile nations. When we start looking at the signs, we need to make sure we separate those prophecies so that we can determine who God is referring to so that we can gain understanding.

Let us turn to the first chapter of the book of Daniel.

Verse 1, "*In the third year of the reign of Jehoiakim king of Judah came Nebuchadnezzar king of Babylon unto Jerusalem, and besieged it.*"

This happened because Jerusalem had forgotten the Lord. They turned from Him and sinned even more than the Gentiles did. Not only that, but they let their hearts harden, and God couldn't get through to them. God was able to get through to the Gentiles easier than His chosen people.

During this time, God began to deal with the Gentile people. I'm not going into all the details of this, but I will give you the results. Daniel, a Jewish man very close to the Lord, kept the testimony of Him alive in his day. God began a great revival among the Gentile nations in Daniel's time. God raised Daniel up to become a voice heard by all in Babylon. Babylon ruled "the world" during Daniel's time, and Nebuchadnezzar was king.

In the second chapter of Daniel, Nebuchadnezzar has a dream that troubles him. He called all the wise men to interpret the dream, but they could not do it. What was so difficult about this dream was that Nebuchadnezzar couldn't even remember it clearly. So, whoever interpreted the dream had to know what Nebuchadnezzar dreamed about. Daniel prayed about it, and God made it known to him. This dream that Nebuchadnezzar had was a vision of the future. This prophecy is for the end times. This prophecy is not about Israel, but it is about what will happen in the later days when the Gentile nations are in power.

Daniel interprets the dream. He tells Nebuchadnezzar that the king saw a great image whose brightness was excellent. The image's head was of fine gold. Daniel told the king that he was the head of gold, for God had given him his great kingdom.

Again, Nebuchadnezzar "ruled the world." His kingdom covered the most civilized part of the world in his time, and he had far more power and authority than other leaders. Much of the world rested on what Nebuchad-nezzar had to say in his day. During his rule, he turned to God and made "the world" worship the Lord. His son turned away from God and lost the kingdom.

Daniel, in the second chapter, talks about four king-doms during the Gentile reign. The fourth kingdom is the last great Gentile kingdom before Christ returns. Let's look.

> Daniel tells us in verse 40, *"And the fourth kingdom shall be strong as iron: forasmuch as iron breaketh in pieces and subdueth all things: and as iron that breaketh all these, shall it break in pieces and bruise."*

This kingdom SUBDUES all things. It BREAKS IN PIECES and BRUISES. It does NOT say this kingdom RULES over other countries. There are ways to subdue and bruise other than military warfare.

> This kingdom is NOT the same as Daniel 7:23, *"The fourth beast shall be the fourth kingdom upon earth, which shall be diverse from all kingdoms, and shall devour the whole earth, and shall tread it down, and break it in pieces."*

The fourth kingdom of Daniel 2, in contrast, does not DEVOUR the earth and TREAD IT DOWN.

This fourth kingdom of Daniel 2 is not Rome, as many say. Rome, of course, did conquer other countries with armies to inhabit them and rule over them. But the Roman Empire is long gone. Rome never was able to influence the world as this last kingdom has done. Why is this kingdom numbered as the fourth? It is not because it is the fourth in some historical sense. No, it is merely the fourth kingdom that Daniel sees. The prophecy stretches from the time of Daniel until the last days. God has revealed enough to Daniel to prove the prophecy and to give us hidden nuggets pertaining to the end of the world as we know it.

Let us take a look at America. It has been called the iron and steel country. America is known as a country that didn't go to war to conquer the world but to defeat the enemy. America has bruised its enemies but did not destroy them and did not rule over them. Does America rule over Germany or Japan, which was defeated in World War II? America helped those countries recover. Did America defeat the Soviet Union? Certainly not in a military action. But there can be little doubt that factors such as sanctions and President Reagan's defense strategies contributed to the break-up of the Soviet Union. Now, America is the only real superpower. What about the situation in Iraq? Is it the intention of America to rule over Iraq? It would appear that Iraq will ultimately rule Iraq, with things like elections and a constitution.

In Daniel 2, verses 32 to 43, the word "clay" is used eight times with respect to the fourth kingdom. Eight times! Then, I would suspect the word has some special meaning. "Clay" is not used once to describe the fourth beast of Daniel 7. God is the potter who molds the clay, as we see in passages such as Isaiah 64:8, Jeremiah 18:6, and Romans 9:21. God tried to mold Israel of the Old Testament like clay to do His will, but Israel faltered. God has tried to mold America, founded upon Christian principles, like clay, to do His will. A "city of refuge" in the Old Testament was a place people in trouble could come for protection (more on "cities of refuge in the next chapter). God molded America into a "city of refuge" and also into a tool to accomplish the Great Commission of Matthew 28:19-20-to spread the gospel throughout the world. Not just missionaries with respect to spreading the gospel, but also bringing certain freedoms to other countries, which makes hearing the gospel message possible.

Missionaries have been sent to the remote parts of the earth for years. Now, the internet is spreading throughout the world. The internet brings evil with good, but one thing that can be said is that it gives anyone access to the Word of God.

According to Matthew 24:14, *"And this gospel of the kingdom shall be preached in all the world for a witness unto all nations; and then shall the end come."* It would appear we are reaching that point.

Another point about the clay is that it does not mix with iron.

Daniel 2:42, *"And as the toes of the feet were part of iron, and part of clay, so the kingdom shall be partly strong, and partly broken."* Verse 43, *"And whereas thou sawest iron mixed with miry clay, they shall mingle themselves with the seed of men: but they shall not cleave one to another, even as iron is not mixed with clay."*

Who is the "they" of verse 43 who shall mingle with the seed of men but not cleave with one another? The subject of the previous verse is "the kingdom," so I would say that the meaning is that the people of the kingdom procreate and have offspring, but they are not of one mind regarding certain matters.

In America, we have races that mix with other races. We have had Italians marrying the Polish and Southerners marrying Northerners despite the Civil War. So what does this "not cleave with one another" mean? I believe it means that America does not follow Paul's message of Ephesians 4 and elsewhere regarding "one body" and "unity of the faith." To me, that is a great weakness of "the church" and thus America. We have all these different denominations who preach differences rather than unity. More than three-fourths of Americans say they are Christians. However, there is no "unity of the faith," and America would not be much stronger. That is how we do not "cleave with one another." We do not cleave with one another in faith.

Now, let's talk a bit more about the fourth kingdom of Daniel 7. In verse 7, we see that this beast devours and breaks into pieces. It is diverse. It has ten horns. The word "diverse" is used several more times to describe the beast, as in verse 23, which I have already quoted in this chapter. The word "diverse" is not used once to describe the fourth kingdom of Daniel 2. We are talking here in Daniel 7 about Satan's spirits taking over nations on earth. The kingdom is "diverse" because it is ruled by supernatural powers, not humans. Daniel is telling the same story that John is telling us in Revelation 13. The beast, in verse 11, has two horns like a lamb and speaks like a dragon and in verse 13, makes fire come down to earth in the sight of men.

These demon spirits cause men to fear them so that they will worship them. The beast has two horns like a lamb, as we just saw in Revelation 13:11. But it is not the Lamb of God, as many believe. America will never be "ruled" by a supernatural leader, as is the case of the kingdom of Daniel 7. Many in the America of Daniel 2 are influenced by Satan, but he does not "rule" the kingdom as he does that of Daniel 7. Folks, I'm not going to go on and on about these verses in Daniel and Revelation. You can study them carefully, pray about them, and decide for yourself.

---

2 Timothy 2:15, *"Study to shew thyself approved unto God, a workman that needeth not to be ashamed, rightly dividing the word of truth."*

The greatest danger to America is not from attacks from other countries or extremist groups. No, America is in danger of crumbling from within. America is in danger of becoming spiritually bankrupt, which makes America susceptible to satanic influences. America is in danger of losing God's protection. What I can only say to born-again believers is that you should support those in political power who try to do it God's way. What would God say about abortion? What would God say about gay marriage? What does God think about prayer being taken out of schools? When some political issue comes up, ask yourself, *What would God say?* And the place to look for the answer is in what God has said to each one of us, in his Word, the Bible.

Although I am very, very concerned about America, I will tell you this: I am proud to be an American, but I am proud to be a Christian.

CHAPTER SIXTEEN

CHRIST IS OUR REFUGE

The most important verses in Daniel tell us the same story as Revelation-victory lies ahead for God's people.

We have been talking about Daniel's second chapter in the previous chapter.

Let's look at verse 44, "*And in the days of these kings shall the God of heaven set up a kingdom, which shall never be destroyed: and the kingdom shall not be left to other people, but it shall break in pieces and consume all these kingdoms, and it shall stand forever.*"

In verse 45, "*Forasmuch as thou sawest that the stone was cut out of the mountain without hands and that it brake in pieces the iron, the brass, the clay, the silver, and the gold; the great God hath made known to the king what shall come to pass hereafter: and the dream is certain, and the interpretation thereof sure."* We see the same result in Daniel 7, verse 27, *"And the kingdom and dominion, and the greatness of the kingdom under the whole heaven, shall be given to the People of the saints of the MOST HIGH, Whose kingdom is an everlasting kingdom, and all dominions shall serve and obey him."*

Jesus spoke of this stone. Matthew 21:42, "Jesus saith unto them, 'Did ye never read in the scriptures, The Stone Which the builders rejected, the same has become the head of the comer: this is the LORD's doing, and it is marvelous in our eyes?"' Jesus is quoting Psalm 118:22, and speaking of Himself, the rejected stone and the chief cornerstone. In Daniel 2:45, quoted above, note that the stone was cut out of the mountain without hands, meaning that this last power, the stone, is not from the earth nor controlled by man. Again, the last power is none other than Jesus Christ.

We have seen the rejection of Jesus on this earth, the rejection of His birth, His Word, and His presence. This last kingdom, called the stone, shall never be destroyed, and it shall consume all other kingdoms. The entire world, including America, will be broken by this last power called the stone. America will not be destroyed by another nation, but God will take America from power. This will happen during the latter days, which are upon us even now. This will happen during the battle of Armageddon.

We have been talking a great deal about Bible prophecy here. Let me give a caution. When there is a worldwide problem or dramatic event, you can be sure it will be in the Bible. At the turn of the century, people were very afraid of what was known as Y2K. Other people took advantage of those fears and sold generators, and dried food, and all sorts of other things to deal with this time of worldwide calamity. I was on the radio at this time, and I stated that nothing terrible was going to happen. Because IT IS NOT MENTIONED IN THE BIBLE, after it was over and nothing happened, the people selling these survival items totally vanished from the scene. I was waiting for all those who sold these things via scare tactics to make some sort of statement, but they all were silent. I believe in the Bible. If people start talking about a worldwide event that is not mentioned in the Bible, I take it with a grain of salt.

In the previous chapter, I referred to the cities of refuge in the Old Testament and said that God molded America into a city of refuge. In the Old Testament, if a person was innocent, they had the opportunity to live and not die by going to one of these cities of refuge. If they were found guilty, however, they were put to death. Many were found innocent after reaching a city of refuge. We all know the stories of people coming from all over the world to America to pursue freedom - whether it be religious freedom, political freedom, economic freedom, or whatever.

This great country of America has helped many people attain freedom. France recognized the potential of America and built the Statue of Liberty. The thirty-foot arm was presented to the United States in August 1876, and then the entire Statue of Liberty was presented on October 28, 1886. It is probably the most well-known landmark on earth and has stood as a welcoming symbol to millions of immigrants for all these years. America began as a God-fearing country and has done many things the Lord's way. But as I have said in this book several times, America is in danger of losing God's protection.

The word "refuge" can be found only once in the New Testament. That is in Hebrews 6:18, where the message is that Christ is our refuge. Is Christ your refuge? He is easy to reach for you. His arms are open to you. The cities of refuge in the Old Testament were places of protection. But they only helped the innocent. The guilty can come to Jesus for refuge.

A while back, my church held meetings in a small town and fed many people daily. It was our intention to provide a refuge for people, not only physically in terms of food and such but, more importantly, spiritually. After being there for a couple of years, the leaders of this community made us close down our church. They said it was unsafe. We were not given any time to make any repairs; we were just told we had to close immediately. When that happened, I then held meetings outside on the church lawn. I was called into a council meeting to be informed it was illegal to hold gospel meetings on the church property. The attitude of the powers that be clearly indicated they wanted us to just leave.

Jesus said in Luke 9:5, *"And whosoever will not receive you, when ye go out of that city, shake off the very dust from your feet for a testimony against them."*

That is exactly what I did, and I went to another place. The first town started off with a good heart and wanted us to feed the needy. We were initially given a welcome and accepted, but then a change of heart occurred. This is what will happen in the last days; only it will be a worldwide rejection, and Satan will lead it. Folks, we need to hold on with all the faith we have. We need to have the faithfulness to continue regardless of what happens.

Continue attending church services, Bible study, and prayer meetings. This shows your faithfulness and will cause your faith to stay strong and be able to withstand the days of trials to come. I have reached a point in my life where I am too stubborn to quit and too old to change, so Jesus, I will continue with You. People, you must persevere in the faith.

When the new kingdom of the stone cut without hands comes about, it will take over the entire world. Man will never again be in charge of running things on earth. The Jewish nation had their opportunity and failed, and the Gentile nations had their chance on earth and failed. Next comes the time of Jesus, and only the redeemed or those who have accepted Christ as Savior will reign with Him. Christ's reign will continue for one thousand years, and then comes the great battle when Satan and all those who follow him are destroyed forever.

Folks, again, I tell you that Revelation and the verses we have been discussing in Daniel show us that only victory lies ahead for God's people. Let me elaborate a bit on the reign of Christ during the one thousand years. Many people have asked me if everyone living on the earth at that time was born again. I do not believe that all people living on the earth at that time would have accepted Him as their Savior. I say this because after the thousand years have ended, Satan will be released for a short season. There will be those who will join Satan to fight Christ. This will be the earth's last and greatest battle.

Just because people live under Christ's rule and under

His blessings or go to His services will not assure them of being right for heaven. Jesus said you must be born again. Every person reading this must have the born-again experience. On the back cover of this book is information on how you can contact me. I would like to answer any questions about salvation that you may have, which I will do to the best of my ability and with my prayers.

CHAPTER SEVENTEEN
ANSWERING OUR PRAYERS

It has been said that more prayers have been answered than this world dreams of.

We pray sometimes and forget about it. A deep, effectual prayer never leaves God's presence without response. If we had our way, we would give everyone everything they wanted. And we would probably be making terrible mistakes. We would probably hurt people more than help them.

Some years back, my mother was diagnosed with cancer. Have you ever heard the doctor say no more than six months for someone to live? That's pretty drastic. Well, that was what the doctors told me about my mother. I called Doctor Fontane and asked about the possibility of her living more than six months. He answered that it was impossible and told me to just face up to the fact that nothing could be done. Everyone was deeply upset except my mother. She seemed to either know something or was learning some deep secret.

My mother remained very happy. Nothing fazed her.

People around her were quite sad, but she kept smiling and said that God had healed her. This was a time of learning for me. I made commitments to God and did everything I could think of to get Him to heal her. Finally, the day came when her entire body swelled up like a balloon. She was immediately taken to McKeesport Hospital. Doctors called for the family to come as they said she only had a few hours to live.

As we came into the hospital room to see her, she smiled and told us that God had healed her. We stayed at her bedside for a few days. Finally, the doctors sent her home and were quite bewildered. My mother lived for more than twenty years after that and didn't die from cancer. She never doubted under any circumstances that He had healed her. I believe she was under attack to make her doubt the Lord. But she stayed positive in her trust in God. I learned a lot from her. We all prayed for her but didn't have confidence in our prayers. We were willing to accept what the doctors said. God showed me something during these times. Never believe man over Him. Never become negative. Never pick bad things to happen over the good. If God had taken her, then we should still be positive in faith. I knew she had a good outlook and stood alone in her faith. When others were throwing out negatives, she kept her faith positive.

Many people get very upset when things go wrong. Remember this: your prayers will be answered if you continue in the faith. If what I have said helps one person, I will be very happy. The story of God answering prayers didn't stop there. My dad was a very stubborn person and didn't believe in this great salvation. He would get angry because I was born again. I could even say that he didn't like me. In the meantime, we were praying for my dad's salvation.

My mother told me something I didn't want to hear. She said to me, "Bobby, God showed me in a dream that I am going to die and go to be with Him." She asked me to take care of Dad. I replied, "Mom, Dad doesn't like me; how can I take care of him?" She told me to do the best I could. About a month later, Mom passed away from a blood clot in her lung.

I tried to get close to my dad during that time. We did become closer, but Dad still held onto his past religious teachings and refused to accept the Lord. He got ill one day, and I took him to the hospital. I kept talking to him about the Lord without getting any response. One day, he told me that there was a very nice nurse who talked to him about the Lord like I did. He said that she was so happy and doing things like raising her hands and praising the Lord. I replied that I thought that was great and left.

The next day, I came in to see him, and he told me something strange. He said, "Bobby, do you know Jesus loves you?" I said to myself, *Dad, I have been trying to tell you this for so many years.* He then told me to get his clothes ready because Jesus had told him he was leaving the hospital in three days. I replied, "Great, Dad, your clothes will be ready to go." From that moment on, my dad was continually raising his hands and praising the Lord. I could hear him uttering the same words that my mother used to say, which caused him to get mad at her.

For the first time, my dad was telling Jesus he loved Him and wanted to serve Him. "Thank you, Jesus," he would say constantly. Three days later, the hospital called me and said to hurry in, that my dad was in a coma. I rushed to the hospital, but Dad passed on before I arrived. Three days to the moment he left the hospital to go with Jesus. I could never reach my dad as a son. But my prayers, along with my mother's, reached the throne of God, and Jesus came down and visited my dad to tell him how much He loved him.

I tell these stories because they are true and may help someone reading this book. God will answer the seemingly impossible prayers if we don't quit. I am going to relate to one more episode. Strange as it may seem, it did happen. This story goes back some time, and it concerns my grandfather. He was Russian and could only speak in that language. I could understand him, but I could only speak a few words in Russian. So many times, I wanted to testify to my grandfather, but the language prohibited me. He did listen to Oral Roberts on the radio. However, he couldn't understand most of it. He lived alone since the daughter he lived with passed away. She had deeply loved the Lord.

One day, we went to visit my grandfather. We found him in the bathtub, but he couldn't get out. Suddenly, my grandfather said in Russian, "I see three people, and they are calling for me to come." He told us he saw his wife, who had passed away many years earlier. He told us he saw Jesus and his daughter Theresa, and they were telling·him to come. He then passed away quietly. The strange thing is that he never knew that his daughter Theresa had passed away. Even when someone cannot understand us, God will get them to understand salvation.

CHAPTER EIGHTEEN

FACE TO FACE WITH GOD

The time is coming when we all will face God. I mentioned previously that God keeps records. The time is coming when God will very carefully examine those records.

Revelation 20:4, *"And I saw thrones, and they sat upon them, and judgment was given unto them; and I saw the souls of them that were beheaded for the witness of Jesus, and for the Word of God, and which had not worshipped the beast, neither his image, neither had received his mark upon their foreheads, or in their hands, and they lived and reigned with Christ a thousand years."* Verse 5, *"But the rest of the dead lived not again until the thousand years were finished. This is the first resurrection."* Verse 6, *"Blessed and holy is he that hath part in the first resurrection: on such the second death hath no power, but they shall be priests of God and of Christ and shall reign with Him a thousand years."* Verse 7, "And *when the thousand years are expired, Satan shall be loosed out of his prison." Verse 8, "And shall go out to deceive the nations which are in the four quarters of the earth, Gog and Magog, to gather them together to battle: the number of whom is as the sand of the sea."*

Those involved in the first resurrection have been considered worthy by the Lord to live forever, and death will never have power over them. Should we not then urge people to turn to God? The earth will be a place of a thousand years of peace. There will be people on earth during this time who will still decide in their own hearts about serving God. However, people will not be permitted to commit crimes or do ungodly acts with respect to others.

Being good doesn't make a person a born-again believer. You can influence people to do the right things, but it's what is in a person's heart that really counts. You cannot force people to have love for each other. Love cannot be taught. Love has to be born into one's life. The Bible says you must be born again.

In the words of Jesus in John 3:3, *"Verily, verily, I say unto thee, Except a man be born again, he cannot see the kingdom of God."*

What are people actually like during this time? After the thousand years are over, Satan will be released for a short while. The devil will be loose again so God can find out who is *really* on His side. Satan will immediately go out and cause a great deception on earth. Gog and Magog side with Satan. These nations will not only believe the devil, but they will also follow him into war against the people of God. They will surround Jerusalem and those who are serving God. They believe that because there has been peace on earth for so long, nothing will harm them. But God will send fire down from heaven and destroy them.

I believe that some people who live during this time of peace and blessings on earth and who have seen what God has done will still not be satisfied. If they have not accepted Christ in their hearts willingly, they still will have a desire to live sinfully. Satan knows that some will still want to take the power back from those who do it God's way in order to instead do things their own way. Satan's plan will never work because God will not permit evil to rule on the earth again.

In Revelation 20:10, we see that the devil is cast into the lake of fire where the beast and false prophet are. Notice that Satan goes directly into punishment. He doesn't get a day in court because he has already been judged to death. In verse 11, we see what is called the second death. And we see that he will be "tormented day and night forever and ever." Would you want to be with the devil?

Let us read the next verses in Revelation 20 carefully.

Verse 11, *"And I saw a great white throne, and Him That sat on it, from Whose face the earth and the heaven fled away; and there was found no place for them."* Verse 12, *"And I saw the dead, small and great, stand before God; and the books were opened: and another book was opened, which is the book of life: and the dead were judged out of those things which*

*were written in the book, according to their works."
Verse 13, "And the sea gave up the dead which were in
it; and death and hell delivered up the dead which
were in them: and they were judged every man
according to their works." Verse 14, "And death and
hell were cast into the lake of tire. This is the second
death." Verse 15, "And whosoever was not found
written in the book of life was cast into the lake of
tire."*

We see in these verses what is called the second death
and the great white throne judgment. God will sit on the
judgment throne. This old earth and the heaven that is
above this earth will be removed or destroyed. Those who
have previously died, the small and the great, will stand
before God and be judged. Only those who have not been
born again will stand at this judgment. The second death
referred to here pertains to those who have died unsaved
and come back to life to face the second death. The second
death means separation from God forever. What death
really means is separation. The books are now to be
opened.

Toe books are opened as the people of all nations stand
before God. One book opened will be the Book of Life. Only
those who are born again will have their names written in
this book. Another book opened is the Book of Remem-
brance. Everything that people have done is recorded. This
is our chance to make sure we make the right choices.
Choose to stand up for what is right in the eyes of God.
Because the books will be opened one day and there will be
no place to hide. There will be the white throne judgment.

In verse 13, we see that the sea gave up the dead in it.

Death and hell delivered up the dead in them. Hell is the place where the sinners were held. Death is a very strong power that keeps people bound. This is the curse that fell upon all men. It started with Adam and Eve sinning. God has always been against death.

Jesus said in John 10:10, *"I have come that they might have life and that they might have it more abundantly."* It was never God's will for man to die. 1 Corin. 15:26 states, *"The last enemy that shall be destroyed is death."*

So, we see death as an enemy of God. We see death and hell cast into the lake of tire. This is the eternal separation. Good and evil will never mix again.

We discussed previously Babylon being destroyed. This was the home of the wicked. The new Jerusalem of Revelation 21:2 is where the righteous will live. It is called the "holy city" and likened to "a bride adorned for her husband." There will not be any weeping there. The sun and the moon don't exist. The light there will be from God's throne. As we see in verse 5, there will be no darkness. No night, no candles, no need for the sun, no death, no sickness. There will be the return of the tree of life as it was in the Garden of Eden.

There will be eating, for in Revelation 22:2, we see that the tree of life bears twelve manners of fruit, one for each month. As manna from heaven was given to the Jewish people to eat in the book of Exodus-angel's food. We hear in verse 17 about taking the water of life freely. Everything in glory is life-giving.

Here on earth, we start the dying process at birth. A

deterioration process begins once we are born. In the last chapter of Revelation, only the life-giving process continues. Everything that is eaten, every sip of water taken, and even the light that shines around us seems to add to endurance and life.

The book of Revelation was not written to make man afraid of the devil. This book of Revelation was written to give us hope. It is to let us know that there is a future and that it is a great future, an eternal future. It only takes us to the beginning of that future, but it tells us the future will never end.

Verse 17, *"And whosoever will, let him take the water of life freely."*

Folks, this is what we have to look forward to!

CHAPTER NINETEEN

FUTURE BLESSINGS

Why did Jesus die? Where will all who have surrendered to Christ end up?

____

Jesus, in Matthew 22:14, said, *"For many are called, but few are chosen."*

____

This means that not all people are going to make it to the place Christ created for His people. We already saw where only those who are born again make it there.

____

Jesus said in Matthew 19:14, *"Suffer little children, and forbid them not, to come unto Me: for of such is the kingdom of heaven."*

____

Jesus has such a great concern for the little children. He

says let all the little children come unto him. They will all be in the kingdom of heaven. It is exciting to know that all those little ones, all those aborted ones, all those mistreated ones, WILL BE THERE. If anyone reading this book has lost a little one, rest assured that he or she is with Jesus at this very moment. Parents who have had a little one pass away, if you are born again, you will be reunited with your child again. There are no sad moments in the new world.

In Revelation 21:1, John told us he saw a new earth and the old earth had passed away. What do we learn in the next verses?

Verse 4, *"And God shall wipe away all tears from their eyes; and there shall be no more death, neither sorrow, nor crying, neither shall there be any more pain: for the former things are passed away."* Verse 5, *"And He That sat upon the throne said, 'Behold, I make all things new.' And He said unto me, 'Write: for these words are true and faithful.'"*

How could it get any better than this? But it will get better as we go on. We will never see another disappointment in this new place where we are going. There, we will not have to wait long to get answers to our prayers. Sorne may ask why it seems as though sometimes it takes so long to get answers to our prayers now. In this world, there is a battle between the angels of God and the devil. Satan tries to prevent what we pray about from happening. God's answer to us is that we are patient. By being patient, we become stronger and defeat the devil. In the new world,

Satan will be powerless. All his weapons of sin will be destroyed forever.

Revelation 21:6, *"I will give unto him that is athirst of the fountain of the water of life freely."*

Energy is increased as we drink this water. There is no need for alcohol because the water will be filled with living energy. You see, wherever God is, life flows. Every move God makes causes life to flow. Everything God makes rejuvenates, and everything is free. Note the word FREELY in verse 6. This is our inheritance, and it is free.

Did you ever feel like you hated for a good thing to leave? Maybe just when you were in the middle of something good, it had to end. The beautiful summer day had to come to an end, but not on this new earth. Revelation 21:25 tells us there will be no night. We will have only light forever and ever.

Perhaps someone you deeply loved died and left you lonely. But not in our new world. We will see our loved ones again and never part. There will be fruit to eat from the Tree of Life. This tree produces a new fruit each month. The word life is used with respect to eating as well as drinking. No more aging. All those who enter here will be beautiful, positive, and happy. All the curses, fears, and sicknesses will be in a place called hell.

I want to take a moment to tell you something that came to me not long ago. I asked God, "Lord, why do we have to live by faith?

Why don't you send people back from the dead to let us know directly from them who have seen your heaven what it is like?" Here's what came to me: if people living here saw what the new world is like, they wouldn't want to go on in this old earth any longer. But God needs them here to be a witness so others will also come to this place of peace. God has told us within His Word about the new world. We have to be perfected because God's new world is perfect.

Now the choice is yours and mine. Do we want to go to this new earth? Do we want our loved ones to go there? Then let's do something about it. Let's tell others about Jesus. Let's continue living. For Him without being discouraged. Let's support the churches that are preaching the way of salvation. If I don't see you here, I will look for you on that new earth. God bless you real good.

CHAPTER TWENTY
DISPENSATIONS

In order to understand the future, you must understand the past. In order to understand the end, you must understand the beginning.

I have used the word "dispensation" several times previously in this book. It is a word often used differently by those who study the Bible. That should not be of great concern. What matters is the last dispensation, the eternal state of affairs which will last forever.

Two definitions of "dispensation" in *Webster's New World Dictionary and Thesaurus* are "an administrative system" and "the ordering of events under divine authority." The word "dispensation" occurs four times in the King James Bible. Let's look at one of those verses.

Ephesians 1:10, *"That in the dispensation of the fullness of times, He might gather together in one all things in Christ, both which are in heaven, and which are on earth; even in Him."*

So you see, it is this, the last dispensation, to which we look forward. But let's take a look at some of these other dispensations.

The man was created perfectly by God and had very few rules to obey- only what God told him to do: not eat of the tree of knowledge of good and evil. Man, however, disobeyed God and sinned. So we see man marred by disobedience. God, being a very merciful Lord and long in patience, lets Adam and Eve go on.

But man began to do what was right in his own eyes. Some, such as Enoch, served God, and some refused to serve God, but God was patient. He gave the man a chance to tum to Him. The wicked crowd, however, got larger and larger while less and less were serving God. God remained patient and waiting. It then boiled down to only Noah's family, who was serving God.

To make matters worse, let's take a look at the beginning of Genesis 6. Verse 1, *"And it came to pass when men began to multiply on the face of the earth, and daughters were born unto them,"* and verse 2, *"That the sons of God saw the daughters of men that they were fair; and they took them wives of all which they chose."*

Because of this, God says in verse 3, "My spirit shall not always strive with man," and he limits man's life span further.

Something happened to make God very, very angry

with man, who was His creation. God saw something so bad that He had to bring destructi on upon the world. These men called the "sons of God," were a group of fallen angels.

They lead offspring with human women, as we see in verse 4, *"There were giants in the earth in those days; and also after that, when the sons of God came in unto the daughters of men, and they bare children to them, the same became mighty men which were of old, men of renown."*

These mighty men were exalted and held in higher esteem than God was.

So God told Noah to build an ark. During the time it took for Noah to construct it, people could repent. But they didn't. When the ark was finished, Noah entered with his family and the animals, and God closed the door. A little over a year later, Noah and those on the ark came out. Ali, those who were against God were gone. The dispensation of Adam and Eve, given dominion over the world, and their descendants ended. It ended with a flood. The waves we have spoken of before being used by God. Now, the dispensation of Noah and his descendants began.

Noah found grace in the eyes of the Lord, as stated in verse 8. Noah started the new dispensation by sacrificing burnt offerings unto the Lord once again. In verse 20, Noah built an altar unto the Lord. There had been a total separation of worldly and Godly. But man again began to choose evil over good. Sodom and Gomorrah turned totally to sin, as did others.

So God found a man named Abram. God told Abram to leave the country and go to a land He would show him. Once more, we see the beginning of a separation from the world. Abram became Abraham, and a new dispensation began. The covenant was eventually turned over to Jacob, who became Israel, and a people who were totally committed to God. But Israel eventually faltered.

God then turned to Moses, who led Israel to the promised land, and a new dispensation began. God gave Moses and Israel the law. From God's chosen people came the strongest man on earth, named Samson; the greatest judge, Samuel; the greatest leader, King David; and the wisest man, Solomon. But Israel again faltered, the kingdom was divided, and many of God's chosen people were driven from the promised land and many others were taken into captivity, or worse.

A new dispensation began with the crucifixion of Christ. This dispensation is marked by salvation by faith and the spread of the church and continues to this day. If you go to Matthew 27, you will see exactly when this dispensation began.

Verse 50, *"Jesus, when He had cried again with a loud voice, yielded up the ghost."* Verse 51, *"And, behold, the veil of the Temple was rent in twain from the top to the bottom; and the earth did quake, and the rocks rent."*

The place called the Holy of Holies was opened, and the secret place of worship was no longer secret. Jesus rose from the dead and commanded the disciples in Matthew 28:19, "Go therefore and make disciples of all the nations, baptizing them in the name of the Father and of the Son and of the Holy Spirit, teaching them to observe all things that I have commanded you; and lo, I am with you always, even to the end of the age." Jesus tells us that He is with us. He is our refuge. And soon, He will gather together those who are with Him to reign forever.

Let's look at some verses in the first chapter of Acts.

Verse 6, *"When they therefore were come together, they asked of Him, saying, 'Lord, wilt Thou at this time restore the kingdom to Israel?'"* Verse 7, *"And He said unto them, "It is not for you to know the times or the seasons, which the Father hath put in His own power."* Verse 8, *"But ye shall receive power, after that the Holy Ghost comes upon you: and ye shall be witnesses unto Me both in Jerusalem, and in all Judea, and in Samaria, and into the uttermost part of the earth."*

So the disciples did. The first Gentile to accept Christ was Cornelius in Acts 10:44. At first, the disciples had been preaching the gospel only to Jews. But at this point, with Comelius, they began to carry the message of Christ to the Gentiles. Israel will ultimately return to her former glory. But the victory will also belong to those who have been born again. Jesus instructed the disciples to witness to the uttermost part of the earth. We are near the time when that has been accomplished, and the next dispensation will begin.

The next dispensation will be the time of tribulation. The Bible tells us that it will be a time of trouble that the world has never seen. Why? Because during this time, man will not rule. Instead, Satan and his minions will be running things on earth. The devil's power will last three and-one-half years, and he will not be defeated by man. Man will only be a pawn in his hands.

Jesus and His angels from heaven will come to do battle with Satan. Ultimately, Satan will be bound by Michael, the archangel and thrown into the bottomless pit. This marks yet another dispensation called the Millennium. It will last a thousand years. It will be a thousand-year reign of Christ on earth. For the first time, there will be real peace on earth. Man will never again take control of the earth. God will be in control. God will permit man to be in charge of cities, but man will not be able to do as he pleases as he does today.

And then we come to the last dispensation, the new heaven and earth, the victory for the redeemed and born-again believers. I have already told you what this will be like. It will be just as we are told in the last chapter of the book of Revelation. Read these words and be blessed. Read these words and know that the time is near. The victory will be ours!

CHAPTER TWENTY-ONE
APPRECIATE BLESSINGS

Many people read Revelation in fear and without understanding.

If Revelation is a book meant to frighten people, then why does it say that those who read it are blessed?

Revelation 1:3, *"Blessed is he that readeth, and they that hear the words of this prophecy, and keep those things which are written therein: for the time is at hand."*

I know I keep coming back to this verse, but it is so important.

My hope is that my words in this book will inspire more people to read Revelation. There are many more nuggets in Revelation than I have written about here. I have not written all the things that I have been blessed to find, but hopefully, many will be blessed with what *is* written here. I will write another book if there is an interest among the readers.

I believe that God is constantly within the reach of His people. God is the same yesterday, today, and tomorrow. How He was in the past is how He is now and how He will be in the future. Our God remains unchangeable.

I want to share a little about an experience I had a couple of years ago. It happened after I was inspired by Hebrews 13:2, "Be not forgetful to entertain strangers: for thereby some have entertained angels unawares." I believed this to be true, so I went out to find an angel. I believe angels can hear not only your speech but also your thoughts. So, I would walk into a restaurant or any crowd of people and think these words mentally. *If there is an angel here, /let me know somehow.* I thought that if it happens that we come in contact with angels oftentimes, my chances of meeting one might be good if I <lid this.

I did this many times without any response until one day when I was in a particular restaurant, I started throwing out thoughts. *If there is an angel here, make yourself known to me.* No one was paying any attention to me, so I just continued to enjoy my food. It was one of those restaurants I liked the best, where you could go back and get everything you wanted to eat. I was on my way back for a second helping when a young man walked up and said a few words to me. He simply stopped me as I was on my way back to the food bar and said, "YOU HAVE A VERY NICE DAY." Then he walked away.

Now, these words weren't earth-shattering, but I will never forget the words or the feelings I had. Strangers don't say that to me. They may say, "Hello" or "How are you?" but never say, "You have a very nice day," right out of the clear blue, at least not to me. Well, this hit me by surprise, and I didn't even answer him. So I quickly ran outside to thank him and speak to him. But he was gone. I looked for a car he may have been sitting in, but all the cars were unattended. There was no sign of any other people around. I asked myself, *Why didn't I say something back there and start up a conversation?* I never will forget what he looked like or the words he said. I believe many of us have been in touch with angels without even knowing it. We need to be more careful about how we speak to people and how we treat them.

Many more blessings happen to us than bad things. The problem is that we remember all the bad things and forget all the good things. A man called Big Jim said to me not long ago after our service, "Pastor, my job isn't fit for a mule, but it's just right for Big Jim." We need to be more appreciative of what we have if we are ever going to see better things ahead. Some people can appreciate helping others, while some don't even appreciate being helped.

Each week, I stop at Tom and Ruth Gravely's house and drop off loaves of bread and pastries that stores give us. Tom and Ruth take it from there and deliver the food to various needy locations. One day, when I brought the food to their house, Tom said to me excitedly, "My wife gets so excited when you bring the food, and she can't wait to deliver it. She immediately starts stacking it all in piles, sorting it the way she wants it to be. She loves to help others."

We help blessings continue to flow by sharing and helping others and by appreciating what we do and what we ourselves receive. Revelation is a book that shows us the end results are going to be better than we have ever expected or deserved to have. Paul said that all the troubles we have gone through cannot be compared to the good things we will have in the future. Keep holding on; you haven't seen anything yet. The best is yet to come. And we should appreciate the book of Revelation for telling us about the future and be blessed by hearing the message.

CHAPTER TWENTY-TWO

THE WORLD'S GREATEST MYSTERY

What is the greatest mystery in the history of this world?

1 Timothy 3:16 tells us, *"And without controversy great is the mystery of godliness: God was manifest in the flesh, justified in the Spirit, seen of angels, preached unto the Gentiles, believed on in the world, received up into glory."*

This book would not be complete without a chapter dedicated to this great mystery.

The world news we watch on television usually shows all the problems without offering the perfect solution. But the Bible is completely different. The Bible shows us where the problem is and then goes on to give us the perfect solution. Let's go back to Genesis. God put Adam and Eve in the Garden of Eden. Then, he told them they could eat every tree in the garden except the tree of knowledge of good and evil (Genesis 3:11). This started out to be a trustworthy place and time for man with God.

There was no mystery here- only complete trust between God and man.

After Adam and Eve ate the Tree of the Knowledge of Good and Evil, things changed.

Genesis 3:24, *"So He drove out the man; and He placed at the east of the garden of Eden Cherubims, and a flaming sword which turned every way, to keep the way of the tree of life."*

Now, we see that the Garden of Eden becomes a place of mystery. Man can no longer enter this garden; man can no longer find the garden. Where did it disappear to? Is there a secret way to enter? How can man find it again?

Only Adam and Eve have ever been able to see this garden. Adam and Eve likely told many of the beauty of the garden, but they could go time and time again to the exact spot but never find it again. They probably spent many agonizing hours of prayer seeking to find what they had lost. Time goes by, and people no longer believe what Adam and Eve say about the garden. The Garden of Eden has now become a mystery. How could a garden, perhaps large enough to be a city by today's standards, vanish from the face of the earth? This is one of the mysteries of the Bible that only God can solve. But what is the greatest mystery of all?

Yes, great indeed is the mystery of godliness. In 1 Peter 1:12, even the angels are amazed at what a wonderful salvation God has provided on our behalf for those who choose Him. A mystery is where you hear something exists, but you can not find it. Many people are sitting in the middle of this great mystery of godliness with no clue how to find the answer. Folks, unless we search for the answer to the mystery of godliness that He has given us, we will remain in deep anguish. How can I find God Almighty? Millions will go on into eternity, never searching for themselves how to find God in their lives.

Some people say that you must experience significant pain in your body to be right with God. Others say you have to sell religious items and give them the money to be right with God. Folks, these ways are totally wrong.

John 3:16, *"For God so loved the world, that He gave His only begotten Son, that whosoever believeth in Him should not perish, but have everlasting life."*

The giving was all about our salvation. I searched for a long time to understand the mystery of salvation. Finally, it came to me. It is no secret to those who desperately want Him. It is only a secret to those who are trying to find another way. It is only a mystery to those who do things man's way instead of God's way. It is no secret to those who sincerely want to find God.

Please listen closely to what I want to reveal to all those reading this book. This is a must, as it is the only way.

Revelation 2:29, *"He that hath an ear, let him hear what the Spirit saith unto the churches."*

If you have an ear, you can hear the Spirit of God. To find God, you and I have to want to find God so much that we are willing to speak to Him personally. God will hear you talk to Him regardless of your vocabulary. You and I must speak to God one-on-one. Go alone and pour your heart out to God. Tell Him you are sorry for all the things you have done wrong. Let God know you desire to live for Him.

Some time ago, I was working on a job with a group of other men. Every chance I had, I would tell them they needed to be born again. Three men would make fun of me and tell others jokes about what I had said. One of the men would start dancing every time I came around.

A short time later, one of these men who laughed and made fun of me got a terrible headache. He went to see his eye doctor. The eye doctor told him he needed to see his physician. He made an appointment to see his doctor the next day. But he died that night. Another of these men had a heart attack. I never got to visit him because he passed away too quickly. The third man suffered a stroke. He had blood in his spinal column and was expected to die at any time. I went to the hospital to pray for him. When I got to his room, I asked him if I could pray for him, and he nodded his head. As I started to pray, his wife entered the room and told me to get out. of there and that they didn't want my prayers. I don't know who she thought I was, but I continued to pray. She ran to call a nurse to chase me out of the room. Well, I finished praying and left before she returned.

I haven't heard anything from these people for several months. But then this man who was supposed to die came to see me. He thanked me for coming to pray for him and said that night, he started to feel better and that God had made Himself real to him. He also said that he would never again make fun of anything pertaining to God. He repented, and God forgave him.

Folks, you can repeat what people tell you to say and never be born again. You can slave to do religious works. But that won't save you. You must accept Jesus Christ and be born again. Someone might ask how he or she can love God. Be honest with God. Tell Him you desire to know Him and love Him. He will send His love into your heart. The great mystery of godliness is that we must experience being born again.

I have not written this book to have people know me. I have written this book so that you may know God. I have written this book so that godliness will not be hidden or mysterious to any of you reading these words. If I don't see you on this earth, l'11 see you in God's place.

CHAPTER TWENTY-THREE

MAKING CHOICES

Most people today want a better tomorrow but don't know how to achieve it.

Remember that your tomorrows and mine are the results of what happens today. For that reason, we need to have a strong grip on God as we make decisions that affect ourselves and others, both now and in the future. The stronger we hold onto God, the less fear of the future we will have.

The new inventions taking place are extraordinary. We hardly get used to a new item when it is replaced by something better. But can all these wonderful inventions compare with what Christ has done? There isn't an invention on earth that can give us peace of mind. Technology doesn't cause love to come into people's hearts, does it? Not one invention has ever satisfied anyone forever. Christ is forever.

Remember this: Revelation shows us that bad things may pass each one of us, but they will only pass us by. Revelation also shows us that the good things will last forever. None of these bad things will hurt you if you get a strong hold on God today.

We are only on the outskirts of the oncoming calamities that will soon hit Earth.

Matthew 24:21 tells us, *"For then shall be great tribulation, such as was not since the beginning of the world to this time, no, nor ever shall be."*

We are approaching a time when not only will the calamities happen, they will all happen at the same time. Why? Because God is releasing his protective hold. When people refuse God, he will leave. People are causing tomorrow to be worse than ever because of their choices and actions of today.

What I am about to say is that I believe it to be true. I wish it wasn't true, but the church of Christ is very weak and spoiled today. It takes entertainment to pull people into church. It also takes things like plush rugs and the best-looking buildings. It takes a popular person to preach to attract people to our church services. To become the person God wants us to be, we need to put Christ ahead of everything else in our lives. Let me go back in time for just a few moments. Years ago, church service started with people gathering around the altar to pray for the service about to begin.

The service itself opened with singing from the heart to the Lord. Individuals at the service raised their hands to call for a song with special meaning to them. Today, songs are all picked in advance for everyone. What is missing here is that someone may have a song that God has placed on their heart. What a blessing that adds to the service! I don't say that it has to be this way in every service, but it can be this way sometimes. This will also present people with the opportunity to feel that they are a vital part of the service. As the music comes to an end, people are excited to testify, giving God honor and glory for what He has done. As the preacher gives the sermon, people are praying that God will lead him to give the right message.

People also will have a great interest in others coming to accept Christ into their hearts. Now, the message begins to hit home, not because of the preacher alone but because a hunger is spreading throughout the meeting, a hunger for more of Jesus. When the altar call is given, people want to respond for themselves and others. People gather around the altar. Some pray for others; some want salvation, some want healing, and some have personal problems. Whatever the need might be, people have compassion and love for each other and the Lord. As the service concludes, joy fills the church. Everyone leaves with faith that something did or will happen because of their prayers. The Christian walk and the gospel service should be joyful and exciting. Only good should be in the hearts of God's people. You can make the choice to make it happen like this for you!

One problem we face is how to know what is true and what is false. The way most people seem to determine what is good is whether or not it benefits them. Another way is to do what everyone else is doing. I have seen in my life that the majority are often wrong. This may not always be true. But I see in the beginning of Genesis that only two people are on earth, Adam and Eve. Both are wrong when dealing with the serpent. Then, a little later in Genesis, Noah builds an ark. All are against him. Only Noah and his family prove to be right. The entire world is wrong. We can't do things in this life just because the majority of people do it a certain way.

We must do things in life mainly with the thought that they are pleasing in God's eyes. Many times in my life, I wondered if I should do something or if it was a sin. I would look around to see if others are doing it. If others do it, then it must be alright to do. I had to learn something very important as I grew up - this is between Jesus and me. What Jesus thinks of me should be the most important thing in my life.

As we look at so many people who have fallen into the ways of Satan, we see that they are much the same as we are. They love some people; they may even feel guilty about many things they do. The problem is that they want to follow the crowd. They let other people do their thinking for them. This happens so often with respect to religion. People don't read the Bible for themselves; they just think and do what other people tell them to think and do. They don't pray personally but ask others to pray for them. It's okay to have others pray for you, but we must know how to get in touch with God ourselves. I have heard this said many times, "Didn't he (or she) say a beautiful prayer?" Prayer isn't a recital. It is talking to God from our hearts.

We live in a real world, but we look through colored lenses when we think of God. God isn't interested in performances. He wants heartfelt sincerity. The religious life of many is all about a show. When they go to church, they must look their best. They go to a church that has the best performance. Who is on stage today? What God is looking for is a person who sincerely wants to be close to Him.

We make choices in this life that affect our eternity. We

can't depend on others to make sure we are right. We must learn that prayer is not a charade. Unless we are born again, we will lose everything when life ends. I would never go to an automobile mechanic to have an operation on my heart or any other part of my body. But some look to people who have never been born again to give them spiritual answers.

I know what I will now say may not be very popular today. Jesus said that you shall know the truth, and the truth shall make you free. If I said things in this book only to make people agree with me, then I would be leaving behind a book that doesn't tell the truth. We like it far better when people agree with us and say things to make us feel good. I know because I also am human. I feel the same way. But if I expect to make it to heaven, I must submit and admit when I am wrong. Pride can block many right things from my sight. It can make wrong things look so right to me. We will make many choices in life. Many will be very difficult to make. I hope we can make the right choices not only for us but also for all those who we meet and love. But most importantly, we must choose to love the Lord and act accordingly as best we possibly can.

CHAPTER TWENTY-FOUR

WHY I WROTE THIS BOOK

All my life I have had a desire to write a book about some of things I have said here. But I didn't feel I was prepared. I did write a small part of what you have found herein once and sent it to *Reader's Digest*. They wrote me back and said I needed to expound further on the subject and then they would like to publish it. I never did respond back.

But now twenty or so years later, I feel I am prepared to tell what I wanted to tell then and much more. For many years, I prayed for wisdom as I read the Bible. I searched for what I call the hidden nuggets of God's Word. What that is are the special messages that are often overlooked.

Slowly I began to find these nuggets one by one that we have overlooked or have been hidden from us. When I say hidden, I mean that we didn't dig deep enough to find the answers from God's Word.

Don't misunderstand me, I still have a lot to learn. I am finding that I can dig a little deeper by praying more before I study the Bible. I am also learning to spend more time with God. Also, I am learning to rejoice when I find my mistakes. If we cannot be excited to find out our mistakes, we will never be able to grow. When God stops me when I am on the wrong path, I thank Him for it, because I can then change direction and let the blessings move into my life.

Another reason I have written this book is because it may help people who I will never meet face to face in this life. Maybe some small word within this book will inspire someone to overcome a problem that has discouraged him or her. Perhaps when I leave this world the words in this book may give someone hope in Christ. Someone may accept Christ into his or her heart while reading this book. Now wouldn't that be exciting?

I feel very strongly that I should share with others whatever God has revealed to me.

Luke 12:3, *"That which ye have spoken in the ear in closets shall be proclaimed upon the housetops."*

If His revelation has blessed me then it may bless one other person out there. Never hide God's blessings from others because the Lord never runs out of blessings. He is a sharing God. The more you share, the more come comes back to you.

There are two types of secrets in this world secrets God tells you which can be shared and secrets which men tell you which should be kept secret. We usually do the opposite. We tell everything we see or hear about others but never say anything about what God has done.

I wrote this book because I believe I have a testimony

that should be heard. I never thought I could remain a Christian. I thought I would falter and not live the life. I knew me, but I didn't know God. I knew my weaknesses, but I didn't know God's strength. Many years have gone by and the Lord has lifted me up over and over.

Many people think like I thought. What if I can't live the life? That's exactly what I thought at eighteen years of age. I didn't think I'd make it very far. And then I will only make God angry with me because of my failure. I am now sixty seven years old and enjoying every moment as a Christian. So I say to all who think like I thought back then-you may know you and your weaknesses but you don't know God's strength and love.

I have written this book to tell you that God has done many miracles in my life and He will do them for you also. Since I first became a Christian all those years ago, many of my family and friends have left this world. All of those family members and friends became born again before they passed away. We are told many places in the Bible such as in Acts 2 by Paul that we will be saved if we believe on the Lord Jesus Christ.

Again, let me quote John 3:16, *"For God so loved the world, that He gave His only begotten Son, that whosoever believeth in Him should not perish, but have everlasting life."*

This is God's promise to all who are reading this book now.

And finally, I have written this book to say this is my way to say I love the Lord.

These are the wonderful people who have made this book become a reality:

Robert E. Faust

Tom & Ruth Gravely William Gay

Arma (Kitty) Wagner Attorney Debra Jackson ValHummert

Robert & Kathy Carnes Joe Wohar

Ray & Clara Reamer BartReamer

Fred & Peggy Hrabak Charles & Elizabeth Toth

Jim Ashbaugh Melissa Krieger

Sam & Sandy Stillwagon to grandchildren Brett, Zoe and Sativa with love

Pastor Don & Joan Amon

Coffee or Tea & Me, WANB radio, Waynesburg, Tom Harris Ministries, Thomas & Eleanor Harris,

Washington, PA Mr. & Mrs. Schwartz Hope Clark

Attorney Tom Rodgers Tony Bukovich

Bob Domin

Rick & Jan Eastman Greenridge, Irwin, PA

Howard & Theresa Suthem, Georgia John & Rickie Morgan

Emily Bauer

Wayne & Alice Kramer Lorrie Pollick

Rachael Hazen Heather Hazen RyanHazen

Dan & Lymari Hazen James Barkley Dorothy Sisler

Robert & Linda Pollick to children Jackie & Stevie

Beverly Pollick Leah Ilgenfritz

Barb Huranik Jessi Pinsky Debbie Jarding Jim Pumell

Philomena J. Reali Mountain Home ID Jamie Pomaibo

Erin Flynn

www.ingramcontent.com/pod-product-compliance
Lightning Source LLC
Chambersburg PA
CBHW021208130726
47988CB00002B/559